W9-BLE-346

craft

of cooking

Notes and Recipes from a Restaurant Kitchen

Tom Colicchio

With Catherine Young and Lori Silverbush
Marco Canora and Karen De Masco

Photographs by Bill Bettencourt

Photogram Images by Bob Dahlquist

Clarkson Potter/Publishers
New York

Text copyright © 2003 by Tom Colicchio
Photographs copyright © 2003 by Bill Bettencourt

All rights reserved. No part of this book may be
reproduced or transmitted in any form or by any means,
electronic or mechanical, including photocopying,
recording, or by any information storage and retrieval
system, without permission in writing from the publisher.

Published by Clarkson Potter/Publishers
New York, New York
Member of the Crown Publishing Group,
a division of Random House, Inc.
www.crownpublishing.com

CLARKSON N. POTTER is a trademark
and POTTER and colophon are registered trademarks of
Random House, Inc.

Printed in China

Design by Bob Dahlquist

Library of Congress Cataloging-in-Publication Data is
available upon request

ISBN 0-609-61050-3

10   9   8   7   6   5   4   3   2   1

First Edition

In loving memory of our grandparents,
Esther Corvelli and Seymour Silverbush.
—T.C. and L.S.

"Make Good Food."   9
How to Use This Book   17

1. meat 29
   CHARCUTERIE   30
   ROASTED/GRILLED   38
   BRAISED   58

2. fish 67
   RAW/MARINATED/CURED   68
   ROASTED   78
   BRAISED   93

3. vegetables 103
   SALADS   104
   ROASTED   117
   SAUTEED   127
   BRAISED   133
   PURÉED   143

4. mushrooms 149
   ROASTED   150
   BRAISED   154
   MARINATED   156

5. potatoes 163
6. grains and beans 179

7. dessert 191
   PASTRY   192
   CUSTARD   209
   ROASTED   218
   POACHED   221
   ICE CREAM AND SORBET   223
   COMPOTES   236
   CONFECTIONS   240
   SAUCES AND SIDES   244

8. pantry 249
   Acknowledgments   268
   Resources   269
   Index   270

"Make

WHEN I OPENED CRAFT *in March of 2001, news-papers and food reviewers credited me with a lot of lofty ambitions, like trying to "educate" the New York diner or to "change how Americans dine." Critics wrote that the menu at Craft was a "maze" and a "challenge" to diners; that I was seeking to unsettle "complacent" New Yorkers, "demystify food," "mystify eaters," and "change the face of American dining." Whew! I was flattered (I guess) but I never really understood the fuss. One reporter asked me, "What was your objective in opening Craft?" pen at the ready for a lecture about my food philosophy. For the record: I don't have a food philosophy. So, I answered: "Make good food." And I meant it. My objective was to make good food. That was all.*

Since I became a chef, people have always asked me what I like to cook at home. I think they're a little dis-appointed when I answer: simple food; some roast fish, a little braised meat, maybe a side of vegetables. But this is really the case; at the end of the day my weary palate craves simplicity. Which is not to say bland food, or even "comfort food." In fact, when prepared well,

good food."

simple food can have an integrity and depth of flavor that fancier dishes may lack. There is something about a great piece of meat, braised slowly in its own juices, the flavors rounded out with a hint of butter. Or a simply roasted vegetable, its sugars intensified into caramel, but still essentially, recognizably, itself. It feels "clean" to me to cook this way; there is clarity to the flavors, a chance to really get at the essence of the ingredient. This is the way I like to cook at home.

When the opportunity arose to open a second restaurant I decided on two conditions: First, the new place had to be in Manhattan close to Gramercy Tavern (Craft is right around the block) and second, it had to embrace something I cared about. I bounced ideas around and toyed with different food idioms, all the while cooking the food I liked to eat at home for my family. Finally it dawned on me. If I loved this kind of food—simple, ingredient-driven, soulful dishes centered around single ingredients (served family-style, naturally)—probably other people would as well. That is, if they could get over the mental hurdle of what "restaurant food" should be.

I started to catalog the types of restaurants where family-style food was de rigueur: Carmine's, a boisterous Midtown Italian-American famous for its gargantuan portions and "dig-in!" mentality. Chinatown, where my friends and family like to order a raft of dishes for the entire group, passing and tasting everything (when was the last time you didn't share in a Chinese restaurant?). I tried to think of restaurants where the dishes focused more or less on single ingredients. Steakhouses came to mind—like the legendary Peter Luger, in Brooklyn—where guests think nothing of ordering a porterhouse for four with a side of mashed potatoes and creamed spinach for the table. All of these scenarios held enormous appeal for me, largely because I was raised in a big, Italian family where genteel portions just didn't happen, but also because, although restaurants like Carmine's and Luger weren't necessarily serving "comfort food," there was something comforting about the dining experience there. Why couldn't a restaurant, I wondered, re-create that kind of intensely satisfying soul experience with fine food? Is there something about "haute cuisine" that demands dozens of ingredients and complicated presentation? I imagine many people would have said yes, but I didn't agree.

So I set out to cook at Craft the kind of food I like to eat, dishes that are uncomplicated but don't lack for complexity. We worked to get at the essence of each ingredient: to make roasted meats taste unmistakably like themselves, only more so, with just a hint of dark sweetness and smoke; to tease out the nuance and character hidden within each vegetable. Textures became infinitely important: the perfect silk of cured fish, marinated just until "cooked" but no longer, finished with sea salt and a dash of olive oil. Or the pillowy loft of hand-formed gnocchi, tossed only in aged Parmigiano-Reggiano and butter, each one a cloud of the purest potato flavor. Sure, it's just a dish of potatoes, butter, and cheese, but taken together and handled simply, the elements sing on the palate and grab you right in your memory center. I don't consider this "comfort food." I guess I would call it "memory food."

Thankfully, Craft has taken off and there has been a subtle but noticeable shift on the part of the press: Where originally journalists wrote about diners having to figure out which ingredients "went together," giving the impression that it was hard work, today they seem to write more about how the food tastes. I guess they're *finally grasping my original intent, which was for guests to order exactly what they felt like eating, with a casual disregard for "getting it right," and based upon nothing more complicated than whim and excitement.*

My goal with Craft is the same as when we opened: to remind diners why they loved mushrooms—or scallops, or short ribs—in the first place. My goal with this book is to allow you the same experience at home. Cook often, and eat well.

Tom Colicchio
New York City
September 2003

How to use

A FEW KEY IDEAS *need to be addressed at the outset of this book. First, if you're reading this, then presumably you're someone we like to think of as a skilled amateur, or enthusiastic hobbyist. Speed and convenience are probably not your first focus here, although they may be your goal at other times (we've all had the experience of needing to rush food onto the table). It's important to recognize that this is a book that sets out how things are done in one restaurant,*

this book

Craft, in New York City. Nothing is being presented as the definitive technique, the "right way," to prepare anything. Rather, these are recipes that reflect our goal here at Craft, which is to make food taste great without fanfare or pretension.

We haven't reinvented restaurant dining at Craft; we have simply pulled the symphony apart and presented a chorus of really great soloists. With this book we try to help you, the enthusiastic home cook, do the same. Sometimes this is merely a matter of choosing the right ingredient: A perfect tomato is ready to eat au naturel, *if you've chosen well. Sometimes it takes hours, even days, to make sauces, stocks, and reductions, to allow* food to roast correctly, or to braise gently to that melting point where meat literally falls from the bone. We're lucky here at Craft; we have some of the most skilled and highly trained graduates from this country's culinary schools, and long hours are part of their job description. Marco Canora, Craft's executive chef, takes this to almost fetishistic levels; he's a determined perfectionist, with a giant respect for food (in fact, quite a few of the dishes at Craft derive directly from Marco's own family repertoire). He and I haven't tried to simplify these recipes for the sake of the home cook. Instead, we leave it up to you to decide which recipes you'd like to replicate at home, and occasionally suggest alternatives. Still, there's no getting around this basic fact: Simple food doesn't mean simplistic. It requires a healthy dose of skill and hard work.

Which leads to the most important point of all. Everything about Craft rests on great ingredients. I would rather take something off the menu altogether than serve it in mediocre form. That's why you won't find exotic items, out of season, that need to be picked unripe and shipped great distances. Or fish stored frozen on a boat for two weeks before it came to shore.

We present food at Craft in a way that is simple and unadorned, because we have the luxury of choosing from the finest ingredients available in the country. We narrow down our choices further by aiming to buy locally whenever possible, so that we're cooking with ingredients that have recently been harvested. The difference in taste and texture is substantial. This book can be a reference guide for your own shopping: Sprinkled throughout you'll notice short, descriptive portraits that offer my take on specific ingredients— what makes the food special, and the criteria I use when buying for Craft.

You may be thinking that ingredients like these are an unattainable ideal, available only to restaurants, but that's no longer the case. The world has changed a lot in the past decade; consumers have become infinitely more educated and choosy, leading many supermarkets and groceries to offer better raw materials. Gourmet shops, many with their own dedicated butcher and fish departments, have sprung up, and they are worth seeking out. Green markets and farm stands are everywhere, where once they were limited to rural areas. In fact, there is a website devoted to directing consumers

to green markets in their own neighborhoods throughout the entire country, so you can buy directly from
farmers whenever possible; I urge you to check out
www.ams.usda.gov/farmersmarkets/map.htm. There is
probably a farmer's market closer than you thought.
Part of this is a matter of changing the way you think
about meal planning. If you're driving in the country
and see a farm stand, stop. Decide what you'll be having for dinner after you've checked it out, not before. If
you're lucky enough to get your hands on something
that's just come from the earth, make that ingredient
the star of your next meal. That's what I try to do at
Craft, every night of the year.

Lots of wonderful items can also be shipped
overnight right to your door (see Resources, page 269).
Although you may not want to buy this way every day,
for special occasions it can make all the difference in
the world. And since you're one of those choosy enthu-
siasts mentioned above, take the time to buy from individual purveyors, wherever possible, over large
supermarkets. Think about this as you would think
about choosing a medical specialist; sure, you could go
to your general practitioner for everything that ails you,

but eventually he or she is going to send you to a specialist. In buying fish, for example, a supermarket will buy a lot at one time, and rotate the old out before the new. This is the most cost-effective way for them to run their business. A fish market, on the other hand, has a shorter distribution cycle. The purveyor specializes in knowing exactly how much he or she needs to buy at any one time, and then does it all over again the next day. Often small purveyors have better sources than supermarkets in the first place (this is key). You may need to walk or drive a little farther to get to a fish market (or a good butcher, or produce market), but you'll absolutely taste the difference.

Whether you're buying at a large market that has separate departments for produce, meat, and fish, or from individual markets, take the time to get friendly with the professionals who work there so that you can call them and order or reserve what you specifically need. They'll be happy to put their skills to use for a consumer who knows the difference, and will often butcher or fillet to your specifications. The recipe for Roasted Cod (page 86) is a great example of how this can be helpful: The recipe calls for skin-on cod, an important factor in holding the fish together so it can be roasted for the right length of time. Cod isn't normally sold with the skin on, but if you call ahead, a good "fish guy" in the market will be more than happy to get you just what you need.

Here and there you'll notice some fairly elaborate "restaurant recipes" set apart graphically from the other recipes in the book. These may be out of reach of most home cooks, due to expense, esoteric ingredients, tricky equipment, or unwieldy size. Of course you're welcome to tackle these behemoths: If you feel like brining an entire pig for Porchetta (page 32), for example, be our guest (and please let us know how it went). I've included these recipes to give you a peek at some of the over-the-top tasks that we take on daily at Craft—tasks that you may be happy to leave to the professionals.

I've also included a Pantry section at the end of the book that sets out some of the more popular and versatile condiments we serve at Craft, along with our suggestions on how to serve them. The Pantry section also holds some essential building blocks—such as stocks— upon which other recipes are built.

Finally, you'll notice that almost all of the recipes in

this book serve six, rather than the standard four. This reflects the family-style service and the quantities we typically serve at Craft. With each dish we try to make enough to go around the table, maybe more than once, assuming that folks will end up sharing. Most of the time we're right. My intention with the recipes in this book is to give your guests the same option, and to assure you enough to feed more than just a few polite appetites.

Designing the Restaurant

TODAY WHEN YOU WALK through the door at Craft, the room gives off minimalist and luxe vibes in equal measure. A curved leather wall draws the eyes back toward a giant abstract horizon by artist Stephen Hannock. Rows of Edison bulbs, filaments glowing, hang in naked splendor, casting light on a deceptively simple design that makes lavish use of noble materials like leather, wood, steel, and stone. To date,

Craft has won numerous design awards, including the top honor from the American Institute of Architects, the "Oscars" of the design world. But it wasn't always thus.

"When Tom first brought me to this space," recalls Peter Bentel, Craft's architect, "it was a wreck of a former print shop. But Tom was an optimist." Tom talked to Peter about his ideas for the new restaurant. "Tom talked mostly

about the feeling, the environment in which he wanted the food to be served. My job in designing the restaurant was to have the design follow Tom's concept of what Craft was going to be."

Peter's design team at Bentel & Bentel set out to collect the best materials available—leather, wood, steel, stone—and let them speak for themselves, in the same way that ingredients on Craft's menu, chosen because

they're the best, are prepared in a way that allows them to stand alone. "We kept everything as forthright as possible. Nothing was hidden behind shellac, lacquer, or paint. The wine cellar was 'hidden in plain sight,' with wine racks of untreated iron that climb to the ceiling. The bar is made of unprocessed steel; the bronze over the doorways and in the bathrooms has been left untreated so that it will tarnish slowly over time." The original plaster pillars had cracked, revealing terracotta fireproofing underneath. Rather than fix the plaster, Peter stripped it away, preferring the natural beauty of the underlying material. Tom likens these choices to the food at Craft, where dishes are stripped of ornamental elements so that the ingredient itself can shine through.

"The menu at Craft is not about showing off the chef, it's about celebrating the food. Our work was not about calling attention to flashy design, but about celebrating the space, the materials, and the craftsmanship used to assemble them." Peter has been especially pleased by the response to Craft's forward-thinking design. "Craft has shown that people will accept modernism, so long as it is warm and inviting."

meat

Charcuterie

Duck ham	31
Porchetta	32
Foie gras torchon	34
Rabbit ballottine	36

Roasted/grilled

Pan-roasted sweetbreads	38
Pan-roasted foie gras	41
Grilled quail	42
Pan-roasted chicken *with chicken jus*	45
Baby lamb	46
Pan-roasted lamb chops	48
Grilled hanger steak *with bordelaise sauce*	51
Porterhouse steak *with béarnaise sauce and roasted marrow bones*	54

Braised

Braised veal breast	58
Braised short ribs	60
Duck confit	63
Braised rabbit	65

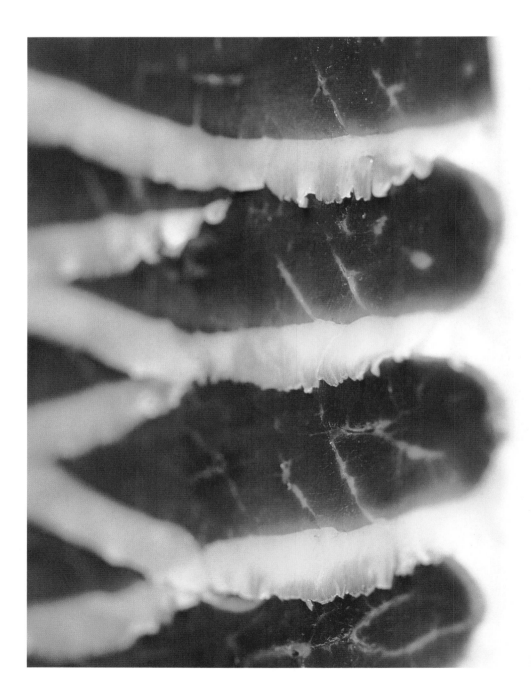

Duck ham

THE DUCK IN THIS RECIPE *is cured very much like prosciutto; it's delicious served with a small herb salad (see page 106) or as part of a charcuterie platter. Hang the duck breasts from the bottom of a refrigerator shelf with some kitchen twine, with a plate or bowl underneath to catch drippings. Unsliced (and untouched), the "ham" will keep in the refrigerator for about a month, and it will continue to cure nicely during that time.*

Makes two 8-ounce hams

2 8-OUNCE DUCK BREASTS

2 CUPS KOSHER SALT

½ CUP SUGAR

3 SPRIGS FRESH THYME

½ TABLESPOON BLACK PEPPERCORNS

1 GARLIC CLOVE, PEELED AND THINLY SLICED

2 BAY LEAVES, CRUMBLED

Place the duck breasts in the freezer for 15 to 20 minutes. Using a very sharp knife, remove the skin and most of the fat, leaving only a thin protective layer in place.

Mix the salt, sugar, thyme, peppercorns, garlic, and bay leaves together in a small bowl. Lay two large pieces of plastic wrap on a clean work surface. Spread about a quarter of the salt mixture on each piece of plastic. Place the duck breasts skin side down on the salt, then cover with the remaining salt. Tightly wrap each breast and refrigerate for 4 days.

Unwrap the duck hams and rinse off the salt mixture. Dry the hams with paper towels, then wrap each in cheesecloth. Hang the hams to dry in the refrigerator for 3 weeks (see the headnote). Slice thin and serve, or wrap in plastic and refrigerate until ready to use.

Porchetta

AT CRAFT, *we prepare a variety of house-cured charcuterie, like mortadella, bresaola, and this rich porchetta. For the most part, these recipes require patience and a lot of elbow grease, but our guests seem to think they're worth it.*

Ingredients	Method
Pig	**BRINING THE PIG**
2 quarts KOSHER SALT	Combine the kosher salt, garlic, thyme, rosemary, and 10 quarts of water and bring to a boil. Allow the brine to cool, then add the pig. Refrigerate overnight.
5 GARLIC CLOVES, PEELED	
1 bunch of FRESH THYME	
1 bunch of FRESH ROSEMARY	
1 30-pound PIGLET, SADDLE BONED, *head and legs reserved for other purposes*	

Ingredients	Method
Farce	**MAKING THE FARCE**
½ teaspoon GROUND MACE	Mix the mace, nutmeg, cloves, paprika, and white pepper together. Combine half of the mixture with all of the iodized salt. Add the diced jowl and fat back. Cover and cure in the refrigerator for 12 to 36 hours.
½ teaspoon FRESHLY GROUND NUTMEG	
½ teaspoon GROUND CLOVES	
2¼ teaspoons SWEET PAPRIKA	
4½ teaspoons FINELY GROUND WHITE PEPPER	Combine the kosher salt, wine, and remaining spice mixture. Mix with the diced lean meat. Cover and cure in the refrigerator for 12 to 36 hours.
50 grams IODIZED SALT	
453.30 grams (1 pound) PORK JOWL, *cleaned and cut in large dice*	Freeze both the spiced fat and jowl mixture and the spiced lean meat for 30 minutes. Run the fat and jowl through a fine-holed meat grinder into a bowl set over ice. Refrigerate. Grind the lean meat into a second bowl set over ice.
453.30 grams (1 pound) FAT BACK, *cut in large dice*	
36 grams KOSHER SALT	
⅓ cup DRY WHITE WINE	
906.60 grams (2 pounds) LEAN PORK MEAT, *cut in large dice*	Add ½ cup of the lean ground meat to a food processor. Sprinkle the meat with powdered milk. With the machine running, add 1 cup of the ground fat and jowl and a cube of frozen milk. Transfer this mixture to a metal bowl set over ice and repeat until all the meat is ground and all the milk is incorporated.
20 grams POWDERED MILK	
2 cups MILK FROZEN INTO CUBES	
3 cups SICILIAN PEELED PISTACHIOS	
½ cup BLACK PEPPERCORNS	Fold the pistachios and the peppercorns into the meat mixture (still set over ice). Mix the egg whites with the diced fat, then fold this mixture into the meat. Chill thoroughly.
5 EGG WHITES, *beaten until frothy*	
679.95 grams (1½ pounds) FIRM PORK FAT, *chilled and diced*	

Ingredients	Method
	Remove the pig from the brine and lay it out flat, skin side down. Place about 3 quarts of the farce in the center of the pig. Wrap the sides of the belly around the farce to form a sausage. Tie tightly at 1-inch intervals, then wrap the porchetta in a large piece of white cotton. Twist the ends of the wrapping as tight as possible and tie the ends.

Poaching liquid

ABOUT 4 QUARTS CHICKEN STOCK
(TO COVER)

3 bunches of FRESH ROSEMARY

3 bunches of FRESH THYME

2 tablespoons BLACK PEPPERCORNS

4 garlic cloves, PEELED AND CRACKED

MAKES 1

POACHING

Combine the stock, herbs, peppercorns, and garlic in a very large pot. Bring to a simmer, then remove from the heat and allow to cool. Place the porchetta in the infused stock. Bring the liquid to a measured temperature of 170° to 180°F. Cook at this temperature until the center of the porchetta registers a temperature of 155°F., about 5 hours. Cool, chill, then unwrap and slice as thin as possible.

Foie gras torchon

Torchon is the French word *for kitchen towel; this dish is so named for the towel or cheesecloth in which the foie gras is tightly wrapped and poached. The final dish here has a wonderfully decadent, lush texture—perfect served with a small amount of chutney, or just some good bread. The trick to getting the torchon right is in wrapping and rewrapping the cylinders of foie gras as tightly as possible, forcing out the liquefied fat. Be forewarned: The final tightening (after poaching) is a messy job, but worth it.*

Makes 2, serves about 12 as an appetizer

1 FOIE GRAS *(about 1½ pounds)*

1½ TEASPOONS KOSHER SALT

⅛ TEASPOON SUGAR

¼ TEASPOON FRESHLY GROUND BLACK PEPPER

½ TEASPOON ARMAGNAC

ABOUT 8 CUPS CHICKEN STOCK

Allow the foie gras to come to room temperature. Carefully pull the two lobes apart. Using a small sharp knife, remove the outer membrane and cut away any green portions and any obvious fat. Working on the smaller lobe first, find the large central vein that joined the two lobes. Carefully lift out the vein and its tributaries with the knife, then remove any blood spots (for this recipe it is more important that the foie gras be well cleaned than that it be intact). Set the cleaned lobe aside and repeat, removing the veins and blood spots from the second lobe.

Combine the salt, sugar, and pepper. Spread half the salt mixture on a plate, place the foie gras on top, cover with the remaining salt mixture, then sprinkle with

Armagnac. Wrap each lobe with plastic wrap and refrigerate for 24 hours.

Roll up one lobe in a clean cotton towel or triple layer of cheesecloth. Form into a tight cylinder 1 to 2 inches in diameter. Twist the ends of the cloth wrapper as tightly as possible. Tie each end with kitchen string, then twist a little tighter; retie. Repeat with the remaining foie gras, rolling, molding, and tying it into a second cylinder. Chill the torchons for at least 2 hours.

Bring the stock to a simmer in a deep skillet or very large pot (the pan should be wide enough to accommodate a torchon). Reduce the heat to medium low. Measure the diameter of a torchon, add it to the stock, and cook for 1 minute for each inch

A sampling of Craft charcuterie, clockwise from center: Rabbit Ballottine (page 36), Foie Gras Torchon, and Duck Ham (page 31).

of diameter. Remove the cooked torchon from the stock. Repeat, measuring and cooking the second torchon.

Allow the foie gras to cool for about 15 minutes, then remold the torchons, twisting, tightening, and forcing the foie gras to expel as much fat as possible. Tie the ends as tightly as possible, then tie each torchon at 1-inch intervals. Chill for 24 hours. Unwrap, slice, and serve slightly chilled. Store wrapped in plastic wrap for up to 5 days.

Rabbit ballottine

A BALLOTTINE IS A DISH *in which a whole boned animal or bird is stuffed with a mixture of forcemeat, or farce. To help the ballottine keep its shape while cooking, we wrap the stuff aul fat, a sheer natural netting taken from the lining of the cow's stomach. As it cooks, the caul fat melts away, glazing the rabbit beautifully in the process.*

Makes 1

For the farce

2 TABLESPOONS UNSALTED BUTTER

1 SMALL YELLOW ONION, PEELED AND DICED

1 SPRIG FRESH SAGE

KOSHER SALT AND FRESHLY GROUND BLACK PEPPER

2 TABLESPOONS EXTRA VIRGIN OLIVE OIL

HEART, LIVER, AND KIDNEYS FROM 1 RABBIT (*see below*)

3 DUCK OR CHICKEN LIVERS

2 TABLESPOONS CHOPPED FRESH SAGE

2 TABLESPOONS CHOPPED FRESH ROSEMARY

¼ CUP SHERRY VINEGAR

For the ballottine

1 RABBIT, BONED (*have the butcher do this*), HEART, LIVER, KIDNEYS, AND BONES RESERVED

KOSHER SALT AND FRESHLY GROUND BLACK PEPPER

5 SLICES PROSCIUTTO

1 WHOLE PIECE OF CAUL FAT

3 TABLESPOONS EXTRA-VIRGIN OLIVE OIL

GREEN OLIVE TAPENADE (*page 261*) (*optional*)

RABBIT GELÉE (*recipe follows*)

For the farce: Melt the butter in a medium skillet over medium heat. Add the onion, sage, salt, and pepper and sweat, stirring occasionally, until the onion is soft, about 15 minutes. Transfer the onion to a plate and wipe out the pan. Heat the pan over medium heat. Add the olive oil, then add the rabbit heart, liver, and kidneys and the duck livers. Season with salt and pepper and cook, turning the meats once or twice until they are firm, about 3 minutes. Add the sage and rosemary, return the onions to the pan, then add the sherry vinegar. Simmer until the pan is almost dry. Allow the farce to cool, then chop it.

For the ballottine: Lay the rabbit out flat, boned side up, on a clean surface. Pound the legs so they are the same thickness as the rest of the meat, then fold them in so the meat forms a somewhat irregular square. Pound any sections that seem thicker than the rest. Salt and pepper the rabbit. Cover it with the prosciutto laid crosswise (from leg to leg) in a single overlapping layer. Spoon the farce into the center of the rabbit. Fold the two ends over the farce, then tightly roll the rabbit. Wrap the ballottine in the caul fat and tie it at 1-inch intervals with kitchen string.

Salt and pepper the outside of the ballottine. Heat the oil in a large skillet over medium low. Add the ballottine. Cook, rotating the ballottine as it browns, until it is golden, firm, and plump, about 50 minutes. When the ballottine is done, a thermometer inserted into the center should indicate a temperature of about 160°F. Serve warm or chilled sliced very thin with tapenade and rabbit gelée, if desired.

rabbit gelée

Heat the oven to 450 F. Chop the bones of 1 rabbit. Place the bones in a small roasting pan and cook, turning them occasionally, until they are well browned, about 40 minutes. Pour off any accumulated fat, then transfer the bones to a pot. Add brown chicken stock (page 251) to cover, about 5 cups, and simmer for 45 minutes. Strain the stock, discarding the bones. Return the stock to the pot and reduce by half. Add 2 sprigs of rosemary, a sprig of thyme, and salt and pepper to taste and allow the stock to cool to room temperature. Sprinkle 1 teaspoon powdered gelatin over 1 tablespoon cold water and set aside for about a minute. Strain the stock and warm it over medium heat. Remove it from the heat and stir in the gelatin. Pour $1/2$ inch of stock into a small baking dish (a 7-inch square will work). Refrigerate overnight. Cut the gelée into cubes and serve with slices of the ballottine.

Pan-roasted sweetbreads

SWEETBREADS, THE THYMUS GLAND *of a calf, have a wonderful texture and a mild, delicate flavor, which works well paired with almost anything. This dish requires some forethought—the sweetbreads need to be soaked overnight—but the extra planning is worth it: Pan-roasting the sweetbreads crisps the outside, while the center stays moist and creamy.*

Serves 6

For the sweetbreads

3 POUNDS SWEETBREADS

ABOUT 1 CUP SUPER-FINELY GROUND FLOUR (*Wondra*)

KOSHER SALT AND FRESHLY GROUND BLACK PEPPER

4 TABLESPOONS PEANUT OIL

4 TABLESPOONS UNSALTED BUTTER

6 SPRIGS FRESH THYME

For the sauce

2 TABLESPOONS PEANUT OIL

2 TABLESPOONS MINCED RED ONION

1 TABLESPOON MINCED CARROT

1 TABLESPOON MINCED CELERY

KOSHER SALT AND FRESHLY GROUND BLACK PEPPER

½ CUP SHERRY VINEGAR

4 CUPS VEAL STOCK (*page 252*)

3 SPRIGS FRESH THYME

For the garnish

1 CUP (*a half recipe*) PAN-ROASTED DICED VEGETABLES (*page 263*)

For the sweetbreads: Rinse, then soak the sweetbreads in cold water in the refrigerator overnight. Drain, place them in a medium saucepan, cover with salted water, and bring to a simmer. Simmer the sweetbreads for 2 minutes, then drain and rinse under cold water. Chill the sweetbreads for at least 1 hour, then carefully remove as much of the outer membrane as you can without tearing the meat.

For the sauce: Heat the oil in a medium saucepan over medium heat. Add the onion, carrot, and celery, season with salt and pepper, and cook, stirring occasionally, until the vegetables begin to caramelize, about 25 minutes. Add the vinegar and increase the heat to medium-high. Vigorously simmer the vinegar until the pan is almost dry, 10 minutes. Add the stock and thyme. Reduce the heat and gently simmer, skimming from time to time, until the stock has reduced by about two thirds and is slightly viscous, about 40 minutes. Strain through a fine sieve, adjust the seasoning with salt and pepper, and keep warm over low heat.

To cook and serve the sweetbreads: Lightly flour each sweetbread, then season with salt and pepper. Heat two large skillets over medium heat. Divide the oil between the skillets and add the sweetbreads. Cook the sweetbreads without turning them until the first sides begin to brown, about 5 minutes. Flip the sweetbreads and reduce the heat to medium low. Continue cooking, periodically spooning off excess fat and moving the sweetbreads, so that they brown on all sides. When they are lightly and evenly browned, about 7 minutes, add the butter and thyme. Cook the sweetbreads, basting with the browned butter and turning them occasionally, until they are crisp and slightly firm, about 10 minutes more. Drain them on paper towels. Wipe out one of the pans and heat the diced vegetable garnish over medium heat. Serve the sweetbreads, sauce, and garnish on warm plates.

Pan-roasted foie gras

I LOVE SERVING FOIE GRAS *at Craft; with very little effort the guest is rendered speechless with pleasure (you just can't beat that). The key to this recipe is to cut the foie gras into thick slices, sear it on a high heat, and serve it immediately; otherwise it will start to lose its fat. I recommend serving foie gras with a small side dish of Mostarda, or mustard fruits (page 257).*

Serves 6

2 POUNDS FOIE GRAS, CHILLED

KOSHER SALT AND FRESHLY GROUND BLACK PEPPER

Separate the lobes of the liver and trim away any obvious exterior fat. Using a sharp hot knife, slice the foie gras about 1½ inches thick. Place the slices on a parchment-lined baking sheet, cover with plastic wrap, and chill until ready to cook.

Heat 2 large skillets over medium-high heat. Salt and pepper the foie gras slices and add them to the pan. Cook until the first sides begin to brown, about 30 seconds, then flip each slice. Lower the heat to medium and cook, basting with melting fat, until the foie gras feels like the thick part of your palm, about 2½ minutes. Drain on paper towels, then serve.

Grilled quail

AT CRAFT, *I like to finish dishes like this one with a drizzle of 25- or 50-year-old balsamic vinegar, which has amazing character and sweetness and the viscosity of syrup. This aged vinegar is very expensive, but it lasts a long time, since a few drops at a time are all you need. For cooking or marinating (as in this recipe) such an exalted ingredient isn't necessary: any good balsamic vinegar from Modena, Italy, will work. Boned quail can be found at specialty butchers or by mail-order from D'Artagnan (see Resources, page 269).*

Serves 6

12 BONED QUAIL

6 TABLESPOONS EXTRA-VIRGIN OLIVE OIL

3 TABLESPOONS BALSAMIC VINEGAR

1 GARLIC CLOVE, PEELED AND THINLY SLICED

1 SPRIG FRESH ROSEMARY

2 SPRIGS FRESH THYME

CRACKED BLACK PEPPER AND KOSHER SALT

AGED BALSAMIC VINEGAR FOR GARNISH (*optional*)

SPRIGS OF FRESH ROSEMARY AND THYME, FOR GARNISH (*optional*)

Clip the wing tips of the quail (for a neater presentation). Combine the quail, olive oil, balsamic vinegar, garlic, rosemary, and thyme in a large plastic storage bag. Season the quail with cracked black pepper and marinate in the refrigerator for at least 12 hours but up to 2 days.

Prepare a hot grill fire. Salt and pepper the quail, then grill them, about 2 minutes per side for medium. Serve the quail drizzled with aged balsamic vinegar and garnished with fresh herb sprigs, if desired.

Pan-roasted chicken with chicken jus

USING TWO PANS *in this recipe allows you to cook the thighs just a bit longer than the breasts, which, in a whole roasted chicken, can sometimes dry out before the dark meat is done.*

Serves 6

For the jus

3 CUPS BROWN CHICKEN STOCK
(*page 251*)

2 SPRIGS FRESH THYME

KOSHER SALT AND FRESHLY
GROUND BLACK PEPPER

For the chicken

4 TABLESPOONS EXTRA-VIRGIN
OLIVE OIL

6 SMALL BONE-IN, SKIN-ON
CHICKEN BREASTS, LOWER WING
ATTACHED BUT TIP REMOVED
(*reserve wing tips for stock*)

6 SMALL BONE-IN, SKIN-ON
CHICKEN THIGHS

KOSHER SALT AND FRESHLY
GROUND BLACK PEPPER

3 TABLESPOONS UNSALTED BUTTER

6 SPRIGS FRESH ROSEMARY

For the jus: Simmer the stock in a saucepan over medium heat, skimming occasionally. Reduce the stock by half or until it is slightly viscous, about 40 minutes. Add the thyme, season with salt and pepper, and keep warm over very low heat.

For the chicken: Divide the oil between 2 very large skillets over medium high. Season the chicken on both sides with salt and pepper, then add the breasts to one pan and the thighs to the other, all skin side down. Cook for about 5 minutes, then reduce the heat to medium and cook until the chicken skin is crisp and golden, about 15 minutes. Turn the pieces of chicken and divide the butter and rosemary between the two pans and continue cooking, basting the chicken with the pan juices. Cook the chicken until juices released when pricked are clear rather than pink, about 20 minutes for the breasts and 25 minutes more for the thighs. Remove the chicken from the pans and allow it to rest in a warm place for 10 minutes, then serve a breast and a thigh with jus.

Baby lamb

BABY LAMB ARE DELIVERED whole to Craft, and then separated into the various cuts—shoulder, loin, rack, liver—by Adriano, our in-house butcher.

Ingredients

1 30-pound	BABY LAMB
8 cloves	ROASTED GARLIC (*see page 260*), *peeled and puréed*
2 cloves	GARLIC, *peeled and chopped*
	KOSHER SALT AND FRESHLY GROUND BLACK PEPPER
5½ cups	MIREPOIX
about ¼ cup	PEANUT OIL
6 to 8 quarts	LAMB STOCK (*see page 48*)
9 sprigs	FRESH ROSEMARY
6 sprigs	FRESH THYME
12 to 14 tablespoons	UNSALTED BUTTER

Method

BREAKING DOWN THE LAMB

Remove, trim, and debone neck, shoulders, and legs.

Remove and trim loin.

Remove, trim, and french the rack.

Remove and trim the front and rear shanks (served on bone).

Remove and reserve the liver.

PREPARING THE MEAT

Rub the neck with some of the garlic purée, sprinkle with half of the chopped garlic, and season generously with salt and pepper. Roll and then tie the neck.

Repeat the same preparation for the shoulders and upper legs.

BRAISING THE NECK AND SHOULDERS

Preheat the oven to 350°F.

Caramelize 2 cups of the mirepoix in 2 tablespoons peanut oil.

Season the neck with salt and pepper. Brown in 2 to 3 tablespoons peanut oil. Add ½ cup of the mirepoix to the pan, cover the meat with stock, bring to a simmer, then oven-braise, covered, for 1 hour. Remove the lid and continue cooking the meat until tender. Cool the meat in the liquid. Simmer the liquid, skim, strain, and pour it over the meat. Cover and refrigerate overnight. To serve, slice the meat. Heat in a 375° oven in the braising liquid. Baste frequently.

Follow the same procedure for the shoulders but caramelize 2½ cups of the mirepoix and cook, covered, for 2 hours. Uncover and cook until brown and fork-tender.

ROASTING THE RACK, LEGS, AND LOIN

Heat the oven to 375°F. Season the rack. Brown on top of the stove in 2 tablespoons peanut oil, then roast, turning the meat once or twice, until medium rare (125°F.). About 10 minutes before the meat is ready, add sprigs of rosemary and thyme and about 2 tablespoons butter. Baste the meat as it finishes cooking. Rest for 10 to 15 minutes. Follow the same procedure for the legs and loin.

SAUTÉING THE LIVER

Season the liver and sauté in 2 tablespoons peanut oil over medium-high heat. Add 2 tablespoons butter, rosemary, and thyme when the liver is flipped. Baste until done.

TO MAKE THE LAMB JUS

Caramelize 1 cup of the mirepoix in 2 tablespoons peanut oil. Season, then add 1 quart of lamb stock. Simmer until the stock is reduced by one quarter to half. Strain, then steep in rosemary. Gently reheat and whisk in about 4 tablespoons butter.

SERVES 8

Pan-roasted lamb chops

AT CRAFT *we use the meaty front loin chops of the lamb and serve one per person. You may find it easier to purchase the smaller back chops. If so, use 2 (or more) per person and ask your butcher to bone and tie them for you. (Make sure he gives you the bones for the sauce.) The lamb stock can be made well in advance; it will keep in the refrigerator for at least a week. The jus could easily be made a day in advance, or you can omit it altogether for a quick and simple dish.*

Serves 6

For the jus

2 TABLESPOONS PEANUT OIL

ABOUT 2 POUNDS LAMB BONES

1 MEDIUM YELLOW ONION, PEELED AND CHOPPED

2 SMALL CARROTS, PEELED AND CHOPPED

2 SMALL CELERY STALKS, PEELED AND CHOPPED

3 SPRIGS FRESH ROSEMARY

KOSHER SALT AND FRESHLY GROUND BLACK PEPPER

For the chops

4 TABLESPOONS EXTRA-VIRGIN OLIVE OIL

KOSHER SALT AND FRESHLY GROUND BLACK PEPPER

2½ TO 3 POUNDS BONELESS LOIN LAMB CHOPS *(bones reserved for jus)*

3 TABLESPOONS UNSALTED BUTTER

6 SPRIGS FRESH THYME

4 CLOVES ROASTED GARLIC, PEELED *(see page 260)*

For the jus: Set the oven to 400°F. Heat the oil in a large ovenproof skillet or roasting pan over medium-high heat. Add the bones, coat them with oil, then transfer to the oven and roast until they begin to color, about 30 minutes. Add the onion, carrots, and celery. Give the bones a stir and continue roasting, stirring once or twice, until the bones are browned and the vegetables caramelized, about 30 minutes more.

Transfer the bones and vegetables into a large pot. Deglaze the roasting pan with about 1 cup of water, scraping up any browned bits that adhere to the bottom. Pour this liquid over the bones, then add enough additional water to cover, about 6 cups. Simmer the stock over medium-low heat, skimming any foam or fat that rises to the surface, and adding water if necessary to keep the contents of the pan covered. Cook the stock until it is nicely flavored, about 4 hours. Strain it and transfer to a saucepan. Simmer over medium-high heat until the jus is nicely viscous and has reduced by about half, 10 to 15 minutes. Add the rosemary, season to taste with salt and pepper, and keep warm over low heat.

For the chops: Heat 2 large skillets over medium high. Divide the oil between the skillets. Salt and pepper the chops on both sides, then add three to each skillet. Cook the chops until the first side is nicely browned, about 5 minutes. Reduce the heat to medium and turn the chops. Cook until the second side is no longer pink, about 2 minutes, then add half the butter, thyme, and garlic to each skillet. Continue cooking, basting the chops with browning butter until they are done, about 15 minutes more for medium rare. Remove the chops from the pan and allow them to rest on a warm place for about 5 minutes, then serve with the lamb jus.

Lamb

I love the flavor of lamb and admittedly have a soft spot for it, because my wife and I were married on a sheep farm on Martha's Vineyard. Clarissa Allen and Mitch Posner, who run the Allen Farm, are a great example of why we try to purchase food from small family farms at Craft; the techniques these artisan farmers use in raising the animals translate to something you can really taste at the end.

Mitch and Clarissa plant twenty-six varieties of grass seed on their farm, a nutritional "salad" that they feel has a profound effect on the quality and flavor of the lamb (one that also, incidentally, has been found to raise the animals' levels of CLA, a natural cancer-fighting agent for the people who eat them). The farmers have devised a system of careful rotational grazing, planting fence posts that guide the sheep to grass that, at four to seven inches high, has the highest sugar levels possible. Toward the end of the growing cycle, the animals are led to graze in a field by the Atlantic Ocean; the salinity in the air is synthesized by the grass, and adds flavor to the meat (in Brittany, where this is common, it's called *pré-salé,* or "salt-meadow sheep"). Compare this to a typical commercial operation out west, where the lambs are introduced into feed lots at the end of their lives to fatten up on grain and inexpensive forage. The grain creates intestinal distress for the animals, so their diet is supplemented with heavy doses of antibiotics.

At every step of the process, Allen Farm sheep are handled with care and respect. Farming this way is a huge amount of work, and a labor of love; as a result they can produce only 100 lambs per year. But their work is an example of why food bought from small farms simply tastes better; it is an early part of the cycle of attention and reverence that continues well into the kitchen.

When buying lamb for yourself, I recommend domestic lamb over Australian and New Zealand varieties; the imported stuff is actually cheaper, but it tends toward grainy flesh, and has to come farther to reach you. Look for deep red, well-marbled meat (although you can expect less marbling than beef) unless you are buying spring lamb, usually about three to five months old, which should have a healthy pink color and a very fine grain. Baby lamb, about four to six weeks old, is especially tender with pale, almost white flesh. In the Resources section (page 267), I've included a list of small, family sheep farms that sell to individual consumers.

Grilled hanger steak with bordelaise sauce

HANGER STEAK *was once referred to as the "butcher's steak" because it was the cut of meat the butcher took home to his family. Although hanger steak isn't considered as exclusive as some other cuts of meat, I love to use it at Craft for its exceptional flavor and rich texture.*

Serves 6

For the sauce

2 TABLESPOONS EXTRA-VIRGIN OLIVE OIL

1 SMALL YELLOW ONION, PEELED AND CHOPPED

1 SMALL CARROT, PEELED AND CHOPPED

1 CELERY STALK, CHOPPED

3 CUPS CHOPPED MUSHROOMS (*such as cremini*)

1 CUP CHOPPED SHALLOTS

1 BOTTLE DRY RED WINE

3 QUARTS VEAL STOCK (*page 252*)

1 BUNCH FRESH THYME

KOSHER SALT AND FRESHLY GROUND BLACK PEPPER

For the steak

3 POUNDS HANGER STEAK

KOSHER SALT AND FRESHLY GROUND BLACK PEPPER

For the sauce: Heat the oil in a large pot over medium-high heat. Add the onion, carrot, celery, mushrooms, and shallots. Cook, stirring occasionally, until the vegetables soften and begin to brown, about 15 minutes. Add the wine and simmer until the pan is almost dry, about 25 minutes. Add the stock. Reduce the heat to medium and simmer, skimming frequently, until the sauce has reduced enough to coat the back of a spoon, at least 1 hour. (The exact time and degree of reduction will depend on the viscosity of the veal stock added; it is best to start with stock that is semisolid when chilled.) Strain the sauce, add the thyme, and season with salt and pepper. Set aside to steep until ready to use.

For the steak: Heat a grill to high heat. Season the steaks on both sides with salt and pepper. Grill the steaks for about 5 minutes per side for medium rare. Transfer the steaks to a plate and allow the meat to rest for 5 to 10 minutes in a warm place. Meanwhile, remove the thyme from the sauce. Warm the sauce over low heat. Slice the steak on the bias and serve with the sauce.

Hanger steak

Each cut of meat that we eat corresponds to muscles in the steer's body. Unlike most cuts of meat, which come as a pair, there is only one hanger steak per animal. Also sometimes known as the "hanging tender," this is the strip of long, thin, fibrous muscle that hangs off the short loin of the steer (hence the name) right where the filet mignon ends, and like the filet, it's a muscle that gets little use. In the filet mignon, this leads to great tenderness but not much flavor. The hanger steak, however, has a lot of marbled fat, giving it a rich, dense flavor—it tastes almost like kidney to me—and a tender, unctuous texture. Because hanger steak marinates well and slices easily, it's a great choice for the backyard grill. I also like hanger steak because it is relatively inexpensive, so you're getting a lot of flavor for less money. Given the choice of hanger steak or flank steak, I'll choose hanger every time—it's much more tender and flavorful, but roughly the same price.

You probably won't find hanger steak in the supermarket (I actually recommend never buying prewrapped meat from the supermarket, if you can help it), but your butcher should be able to get it for you, especially if you call ahead. We like to serve it at Craft and at Craftsteak, in Las Vegas, as a flavorful, interesting alternative to popular favorites like New York strip or porterhouse.

Porterhouse steak with béarnaise sauce and roasted marrow bones

PORTERHOUSE STEAKS *are especially prized by steak lovers because each one includes both a piece of the richly marbled strip, or short loin, and the tenderloin, which translates to heavy-duty flavor. When buying, look for dry-aged steaks (the loss of moisture in aging concentrates the flavor even further) that are about 2 inches thick. This recipe intentionally makes only a small amount of sauce; it's so rich you won't need more than 2 to 3 tablespoons per person.*

Serves 4

For the sauce

¾ CUP PLUS 2 TABLESPOONS DRY WHITE WINE

¾ CUP WHITE WINE VINEGAR

3 SHALLOTS, PEELED AND THINLY SLICED

MARROW FROM 1 BEEF MARROW BONE *(optional, see note)*

4 SPRIGS FRESH TARRAGON

2 EGG YOLKS

½ CUP CLARIFIED BUTTER, WARM *(page 195)*

¼ CUP HEAVY CREAM, WHIPPED

1 TABLESPOON FRESHLY CHOPPED TARRAGON

KOSHER SALT AND FRESHLY GROUND BLACK PEPPER

For the steaks

4 TABLESPOONS PEANUT OIL

KOSHER SALT AND FRESHLY GROUND BLACK PEPPER

2 2-INCH-THICK, 24-OUNCE PORTERHOUSE STEAKS

4 TABLESPOONS UNSALTED BUTTER

3 SPRIGS FRESH THYME

3 SPRIGS FRESH ROSEMARY

6 MARROW BONES

For the sauce: Combine the wine, vinegar, shallots, marrow (if using), and tarragon in a saucepan. Bring to a boil over high heat and reduce until only 2 to 3 tablespoons of liquid remain, about 15 minutes. Press the reduction through a fine sieve into a bowl and set aside.

For the steaks: Heat the oven to 200°F. Divide the oil between 2 large skillets and heat over medium. Salt and pepper the steaks on both sides and add them to the pans. Cook the steaks until the first sides are nicely browned, 7 to 10 minutes.

Turn the steaks and add the butter, thyme, rosemary, and marrow bones. Cook, basting the steaks with the herb butter and turning the marrow bones so they color on all sides, about 10 minutes more for medium rare.

Transfer the steaks to a platter and the bones to the oven. Pour the pan juices over the steaks and let rest in a warm place for about 10 minutes. Continue cooking the bones just until heated through, about 10 minutes. Meanwhile, finish the sauce.

Whisk the egg yolks in a metal bowl until they froth and begin to have some body. Set the bowl over a pot filled with water heated to just below a simmer. Add the reduction to the yolks and beat with a wooden spoon until the mixture thickens enough so the spoon leaves a trail. Remove the bowl from the heat and gradually beat in the warm clarified butter. While stirring, warm the sauce over the pan of hot water, then fold in the whipped cream. Add the chopped tarragon and season with salt and pepper.

Slice the steaks and serve with the bones and sauce.

Note

Adding marrow to béarnaise gives it a richer flavor. Soak the bone in heavily salted water overnight (this forces the blood from the marrow). Drain the bone, then spoon out the marrow. Combine it with the wine, vinegar, shallots, and tarragon as directed above.

Receiving and Prep

August 23
7:00 A.M.

IT'S A STEAMY AUGUST morning, and the trucks rumble and clank along the pitted street of Manhattan's Flatiron District, coming to a stop at 43 East 19th Street. In the space of a couple of hours a procession of food, crates of colorful vegetable symmetry, of fins and scales, glinting bones and marbled meat, will be wheeled off the trucks and into Craft. Emilio, a tall Dominican, stands by the service elevator, checking every new delivery against a list. He rips open a crate of sugar snap peas and fingers them, snapping one in two. He pops both halves into his mouth, chews. Nods. The crates are wheeled past him to the walk-in. Next in are flat cartons of figs, little dusky moons peeking out between the cardboard flaps. They, too, are prodded, assessed. Then five crates of Jerusalem artichokes arrive on a hand truck looking like knobby, mutant potatoes. It seems sufficient for a month, but in reality these should last through tonight's dinner (maybe). Tomorrow another five

crates will arrive, and then five more the day after that. As ingredients appear they peel off left and right to prep cooks, to storerooms, and to the walk-in. Everyone moves quickly, with a calm haste born of practice and the approaching deadline of lunch.

Within minutes, two fifty-pound sacks of onions, five cases of pinot noir (2000 Foley, from Santa Maria), five crates of white corn (four dozen ears to a crate), and six warm sacks of fresh bread appear, a wafting yeasty scent trailing the man from Tom Cat Bakery. Emilio directs the placement of each delivery into the packed walk-in—a feat of the most efficient feng shui ever seen—and then, impossibly, finds even more space for eight boxes of prime ribs, strip loins, ground veal, and extra stock bones. Everything is touched or tasted, sniffed, petted, poked, counted, squeezed. Anything found less than perfect will go back onto the truck, but it doesn't happen often. A closer look and it's clear why; the ingredients com-

ing through the door are insanely robust, possessed of an almost embarrassing ripeness and color, like the supermarket versions' bionic cousins. It helps, too, that it is the end of August: Tomatoes are in riotous form, as are zucchini, corn, berries, herbs, you name it. It's an exuberant time of year for produce, and an important season for a restaurant like Craft, which builds its entire mission around the quality and variety of great, local food. When a flat of blackberries is hoisted from the service elevator to Karen, in pastry, she picks one up and tastes it, shaking her head, in awe. "These are so gorgeous, I almost don't want to cook with them," she says, and whisks them off to become a tart, a batch of sorbet, or nothing at all but a dish of blackberries, unadorned and complete, if that's what your guests desire.

A forty-three-pound halibut, twice the length of a man's arm, is wheeled through the door. Emilio looks at its eyes, bright and unclouded, touches the

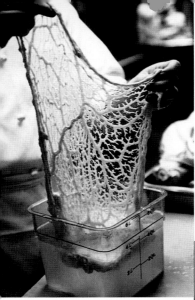

fins, the gills, presses the flesh with his hands and smells. He nods and the mammoth creature is laid out on the block. Adriano, fluent in Spanish and in fishmonger's shorthand, picks up a knife with a menacing curve and gets to work, cleaning, scaling. Fillets appear, pearly and clean, as the knife travels the length of the fish; scales, fins, and bones become a loose heap scraped to one side. Someone appears and wordlessly makes off with the fillets. Adriano cleans off his knife, wipes down the board, and grabs a monkfish next. It's the ugliest thing you've ever seen, but a favorite among the cooks for its rich texture and versatility. In short order it, too, is reduced to clean fillets, a hollow of bone dimpling the center of each.

A crate of lobsters is next through the door. P.J., a new cook, leaves his cutting board long enough to feed them one by one into a massive pot of boiling water. "We parboil them, then I'll separate the tails and claws from the bodies. These should get us through service today, and then I'll use the shells for lobster stock." After three minutes the lobsters are plunged into a trough of ice water. P.J. turns just long enough to stir a pan of butter that melts quietly over gentle heat; as the water evaporates he will skim off the solids and give the clarified remains to pastry for baking, and then he's back to his board, dicing carrots and celery for mirepoix. Another young cook ladles a heap of jellied veal stock into a pot, where it will melt down and become the braising liquid for short ribs. "This here's one hundred pounds of beef ribs," he says, nodding at slabs of ribs that are marinating in a pungent bath of merlot and fresh herbs. "I'll braise them in the veal stock for about six hours or so. We'll go through these in a day, maybe two, so I'll braise a batch like this about four, five times a week." In the winter the cooks will braise 100 pounds of short ribs every day, and still won't be able to keep up with the demand.

This meat, as well as the porterhouses and strip steaks, come from Jobaggy, a family-run operation with a direct pipeline to limited stores of Prime USDA, usually earmarked for the great steakhouses. "To serve meat of this quality, you have to be willing to charge for it," says Tom, watching the boxes wheel through the door. "It's so expensive, it's tempting to serve something else, at a more gentle price point, just to keep the guest happy." And yet, Craft's diners seem to understand that they're getting ingredients that are scarce or singular. "I think once they taste a real diver scallop—that incredible sweetness when it's caught a couple hours ago—or a piece of day-boat fish, or meat like this, something 'clicks' for them, and then the prices make sense." He grins. "At least, I hope so." While he ruminates on this, the service elevator starts to clank and wheeze once again, and another truck pulls up, ready to release the treasures inside.

Braised veal breast

ALLOW PLENTY OF TIME *for this recipe; the veal should be served at least a day after it is braised (this allows it to firm up sufficiently to be sliced into neat rounds). Besides, like most braises, the flavors are better a day or two after it's made. Any extra braising sauce can be kept warm and passed separately to be spooned over the veal, or used as an excellent, richly flavored sauce for pasta.*

Serves 6

4 GARLIC CLOVES, PEELED

1 3- TO 4-POUND BONELESS
VEAL BREAST (*half of a large breast*),
BONES RESERVED
FOR STOCK

FRESHLY GROUND BLACK PEPPER
AND KOSHER SALT

3 TABLESPOONS PEANUT OIL

1 LARGE ONION, PEELED AND
CHOPPED

1 LARGE CARROT, PEELED AND
CHOPPED

3 CELERY STALKS, CHOPPED

2 CUPS DRY WHITE WINE

6 SPRIGS FRESH ROSEMARY

ABOUT 8 CUPS VEAL STOCK
(*page 252*)

¼ CUP BLONDE SOFFRITTO BASE
(*page 255*)

1 TEASPOON TOMATO PASTE

2 WHOLE, PEELED TOMATOES
(*fresh or canned*)

MINCED ZEST OF 1 LEMON

Heat the oven to 350°F. Wrap the garlic in aluminum foil and roast until soft, about 30 minutes. Remove the garlic from the oven and allow it to cool.

Meanwhile, lay the veal flat. Smash the roasted garlic and spread it over the veal. Season with black pepper, then roll the veal and tie it tightly at 2-inch intervals with kitchen string. Generously salt and pepper the veal roll.

Heat the oil in a large, high-sided oven-proof skillet or Dutch oven over medium-high heat. Add the veal and brown on all sides, 30 to 40 minutes. Remove the veal, reduce the heat to medium, and add the onion, carrot, and celery. Season the vegetables with salt and pepper and cook, stirring occasionally, until they begin to brown, about 20 minutes. Add the wine and 4 sprigs of the rosemary and bring to a simmer. Return the veal to the pan. Add enough stock to just cover the veal and bring it to a simmer. Cover the pot and transfer it to the oven. Braise at a very gentle simmer, lowering the heat if necessary, for 2 hours. Remove the lid and continue gently simmering, skimming frequently and turning the meat once or twice, until the veal is very tender, another hour or so. Remove the pot from the oven and allow the veal to cool in the braising liquid. When it is cool, ladle the braising liquid through a fine sieve into a pot. Bring it to a simmer over medium-high heat. Skim the liquid, then pour it over the veal. Cover the veal and refrigerate overnight.

To serve, cook the soffritto in a skillet over medium heat, stirring frequently, until it is quite dark, about 40 minutes. Meanwhile, lift the veal out of the braising liquid.

Wrap the veal in plastic and refrigerate while the sauce cooks. Reduce the braising liquid by about half, until it is very slightly viscous. Add the tomato paste and the remaining 2 sprigs of rosemary to the soffritto. Cook until the tomato darkens, 3 to 5 minutes, then add the reduced stock and the tomatoes, breaking them up with your hands or the back of a spoon. Add the lemon zest and allow the mixture to simmer gently over medium-low heat until the flavors blend, about 20 minutes.

Heat the oven to 375°F. Slice the veal into six equal pieces. Place the slices in a single layer in a small roasting pan or large baking dish. Add enough of the sauce to the pan to come about two thirds of the way up the meat. Simmer in the oven, basting frequently, until the meat is nicely glazed, about 20 minutes, then serve.

Braised short ribs

THE BRAISED SHORT RIBS *at Craft are a huge favorite; we go through almost 500 pounds a week! This is a make-ahead recipe; most braises are better the day after they've cooked, since the flavors will continue to develop. The important thing is to store the short ribs in their braising liquid, or they will dry out. Cut away the rib bones before reheating; they will be easy to remove from the chilled meat.*

Serves 6

For the marinade

2 TABLESPOONS PEANUT OIL

6 10-OUNCE BEEF SHORT RIBS

KOSHER SALT AND FRESHLY GROUND BLACK PEPPER

2 SMALL YELLOW ONIONS, PEELED AND CHOPPED

2 SMALL CARROTS, PEELED AND CHOPPED

3 CELERY STALKS, CHOPPED

3 GARLIC CLOVES, PEELED

1 BOTTLE DRY RED WINE

1 SMALL BUNCH FRESH THYME

For the braise

2 TABLESPOONS PEANUT OIL

2 SMALL YELLOW ONIONS, PEELED AND CHOPPED

2 SMALL CARROTS, PEELED AND CHOPPED

3 CELERY STALKS, CHOPPED

3 GARLIC CLOVES, PEELED

KOSHER SALT AND FRESHLY GROUND BLACK PEPPER

1 SMALL BUNCH FRESH THYME

2 TO 3 CUPS VEAL STOCK *(page 252)* OR BROWN CHICKEN STOCK *(page 251)*

For the marinade: Heat the oil in a large skillet over medium heat. Season the ribs with salt and pepper and brown them in batches on all sides, about 40 minutes per batch. Remove the ribs from the skillet and place them bone side down in a single layer in a baking dish or large container. Add the onions, carrots, and celery stalks to the skillet. Add the garlic, season with salt and pepper, and cook, stirring occa-

sionally, until the vegetables are tender and golden, about 30 minutes. Pour in the wine and add the thyme. Bring the marinade to a boil, then remove it from the heat. Pour the warm marinade over the meat. Cover and refrigerate for 12 to 24 hours, turning the ribs at least once.

For the braise: Drain the ribs, reserving the wine but discarding the vegetables and

(Continued)

herbs. Set the oven to 350°F. Heat the oil in a very large, high-sided ovenproof skillet or other braising pan over medium heat. Add the onions, carrots, celery, garlic, and salt and pepper to taste. Sweat the vegetables, stirring occasionally, for about 20 minutes.

Meanwhile, bring the wine to a boil in a saucepan and skim any foam that rises to the surface. When the vegetables are tender add the thyme, ribs, wine, and enough stock to barely cover. Bring the stock to a simmer, then cover the pan and transfer it to the oven.

Braise the meat in the oven at a very gentle simmer (tiny bubbles) for 1½ hours, then remove the lid. Continue simmering, adjusting the oven temperature if necessary and basting occasionally, until the meat is fork tender, about 1½ hours longer. Allow the ribs to cool slightly, then remove them from the pot. Strain and degrease the braising liquid. Place the ribs in a shallow container, pour the liquid over them, and refrigerate overnight.

To serve, heat the oven to 350°F. Remove the ribs from the braising liquid. Separate the meat from the bones (use a knife to ensure a neat presentation). Discard the bones and place the meat in an ovenproof serving pan. Bring the braising liquid to a boil in a saucepan. Then, pour enough of it over the ribs to come about halfway up them. Heat the ribs in the oven, basting frequently with the reducing braising liquid. Continue cooking and basting until the meat is heated through and nicely glazed, about 40 minutes.

Duck confit

CONFIT IS A FRENCH TERM *for "preserve"; it was originally devised as a way of slow-cooking and then preserving poultry or meat in its own fat. Today we make confit purely for its flavor, but it will keep conveniently in the fridge for up to 2 weeks. At Craft we serve Duck Confit with a garnish of diced pan-roasted vegetables. See Resources, page 269, for suggestions on purchasing duck fat.*

Makes 6

2 CUPS KOSHER SALT

½ CUP SUGAR

2 TABLESPOONS BLACK PEPPERCORNS

2 GARLIC CLOVES, PEELED AND SLICED

6 LARGE DUCK LEGS WITH THIGHS

1 BUNCH OF FRESH THYME

ABOUT 5 CUPS DUCK FAT

PAN-ROASTED DICED VEGETABLES *(page 263)*, OPTIONAL

Combine the salt, sugar, peppercorns, and garlic. Spread half of the mixture in the bottom of a baking dish large enough to hold the duck legs in a single layer. Arrange half the thyme on the salt mixture, then place the duck, skin side up, on top. Cover the duck first with the remaining thyme and then with the remaining salt mixture. Cover the baking dish and refrigerate for 12 hours.

Rinse off the legs, then dry them. Place them in a large pot. Melt enough duck fat to cover the legs. Pour the fat over the duck. Bring the contents of the pot to a simmer over medium heat. Reduce the heat to low, cover, and cook until the meat

begins to separate from the bone, about 2¹/₂ hours. Cool and store the confit in the fat.

To serve, heat the oven to 400°F. Melt the fat and remove the legs (the fat can be reused). Heat a large, nonstick ovenproof skillet over medium-high heat. Add the duck, skin side down. Cook until the pan is once again hot, about 2 minutes, then cover the skillet and transfer it to the oven. Cook until the skin is crisp, 8 to 12 minutes, then turn the duck legs and cook over medium heat for 1 minute longer. Warm the diced vegetables, if using, and serve.

Braised rabbit

THIS STRAIGHTFORWARD *braising recipe would also work well with chicken, beef, or lamb. Note that unless you have a very large pan, it may be necessary to divide the vegetable, tomato, and wine mixture between two pans before adding the rabbit and the stock.*

Serves 6

3 TABLESPOONS EXTRA-VIRGIN OLIVE OIL, PLUS ADDITIONAL FOR GARNISH

KOSHER SALT AND FRESHLY GROUND BLACK PEPPER

3 RABBITS (*have the butcher separate the front legs, loins, and back legs, leaving all on the bone*)

1 RED ONION, PEELED AND MINCED

1 CELERY STALK, MINCED

1 MEDIUM CARROT, PEELED AND MINCED

2 CUPS DRY WHITE WINE

10 WHOLE, PEELED PLUM TOMATOES (*canned or fresh*)

6 SPRIGS FRESH ROSEMARY

1 CUP PITTED NIÇOISE OLIVES

ABOUT 6 CUPS BROWN CHICKEN STOCK (*page 251*)

3 TABLESPOONS FINELY CHOPPED FRESH FLAT-LEAF PARSLEY (*optional*)

MINCED ZEST OF 1 LEMON (*optional*)

Heat the oven to 350°F. Heat a large, high-sided ovenproof skillet over medium heat. Add the oil. Salt and pepper the rabbit and add to fill but not crowd the pan. Brown on both sides, about 20 minutes in all, then transfer to a plate. Repeat until all the rabbit has been browned.

Add the onion, celery, carrot, and salt and pepper to the pan. Cook, stirring occasionally, until the vegetables are tender and nicely browned, about 30 minutes. Pour in the wine and reduce by about half. Add the tomatoes, breaking them up with

your hands or a wooden spoon, then add the rosemary and olives. Cook for a minute or so, then fit the rabbit snugly into the pan. Add enough stock to not quite cover the rabbit and bring to a simmer.

Transfer the pan to the oven and braise, uncovered, at a slow bubble. Cook the rabbit, turning it once or twice, until it is so tender it almost falls from the bone, about 1½ hours. Degrease the braising liquid if necessary and serve the rabbit with the chopped parsley mixed with lemon zest and a little olive oil.

fish

2.

Raw/marinated/cured

Cured yellowtail (hamachi)   68
with lemon-coriander vinaigrette

Cured arctic char   71

Pickled sardines   73

Grilled squid   75

Sea urchin   76
with fennel purée

Roasted

Roasted sea scallops   78
with scallop jus

Pan-roasted soft-shell crabs   80

Pan-roasted skate   85

Roasted cod   86

Sturgeon   89
wrapped in prosciutto

Braised

Lobster   93
braised in beurre fondue

Braised red snapper   95

Braised monkfish   96

Braised striped bass   98

Cured yellowtail (hamachi) with lemon-coriander vinaigrette

FOLKS OFTEN CONFUSE *this fish with yellowfin tuna, but hamachi is actually yellowtail jack, a fish in the same family as pompano. This dish is a particularly popular starter at Craft; many people are comfortable with hamachi, since they've eaten it raw at sushi bars. Use the freshest possible fish here; it will taste and feel clean and silky on the palate. Unfortunately hamachi can sometimes be hard to find (see Resources, page 269, for possible sources); if that's the case, you can substitute striped bass or any other firm, white, just-out-of-the-water-fresh fish.*

Makes 2 pounds

For the fish

6 TABLESPOONS CORIANDER SEEDS

1½ CUPS KOSHER SALT

¼ CUP SUGAR

2 POUNDS YELLOWTAIL FILLET, SKINNED AND DARK (*blood-stained*) PORTIONS TRIMMED

2 TABLESPOONS CHOPPED FRESH LEMON VERBENA (*or 1 tablespoon minced lemon zest*)

1 TABLESPOON CHOPPED FRESH LEMON THYME (*or 1 tablespoon fresh thyme*)

1 LEMON, VERY THINLY SLICED

For the vinaigrette

¼ CUP CHAMPAGNE VINEGAR

KOSHER SALT AND FRESHLY GROUND BLACK PEPPER

2 TABLESPOONS CHOPPED LEMON CONFIT (*page 258*)

6 TABLESPOONS EXTRA-VIRGIN OLIVE OIL

LEMON OIL (*optional*)

For the fish: Heat the oven to 350°F. Toast the coriander seeds on a baking sheet in the oven until fragrant, 10 to 15 minutes. Using a rolling pin, lightly crush the seeds. Reserve 2 tablespoons for the vinaigrette.

To cure the fish, mix ¼ cup of the coriander seeds, the salt, and the sugar together, then lay half of this mixture on a large sheet of plastic wrap. Lay the fish skinned side down on the salt mixture. Mix the herbs together and spread them over the fish, top with the lemon slices, then cover with the remaining salt mixture. Wrap the fish tightly in a triple layer of plastic wrap, place it on a plate, and top it with a second plate. Weight the fish (place cans on the top plate), then refrigerate for 3 hours.

Unwrap the fish and brush off the salt mixture. Gently rinse the fish; it will be slightly firm but still nearly raw. Wrap the fish in clean plastic and refrigerate until ready to serve.

For the vinaigrette: Season the vinegar with salt and pepper and add the reserved coriander seeds and the lemon confit. Gradually whisk in the olive oil.

To serve, slice the fish about 1/4 to 1/2 inch thick. Arrange the slices on chilled plates. Drizzle with the vinaigrette and with lemon oil, if desired.

Cured arctic char

SALT CURES WERE *traditionally used to preserve fish for an extended period of time. At Craft I like to cure fish quickly as a way to add flavor and firm up the texture; long-term preservation is no longer the goal. Char is an ideal choice; it has a similar color and texture to salmon, but unlike salmon, the fillets are small. You can cure the fish and eat the whole thing without the leftovers over-curing and becoming too salty in the following days.*

Makes 1 pound

1 1-POUND FILLET OF ARCTIC CHAR

1 CUP BROWN SUGAR

2 CUPS KOSHER SALT

1 SMALL FENNEL BULB, CORED AND VERY THINLY SHAVED

2 TABLESPOONS CHOPPED FRESH FLAT-LEAF PARSLEY

1 TABLESPOON CHOPPED FRESH CHERVIL

1 TABLESPOON CHOPPED FRESH TARRAGON

2 TABLESPOONS CORIANDER SEEDS, TOASTED

2 TABLESPOONS FENNEL SEEDS

½ TEASPOON CRACKED WHITE PEPPER

MINCED ZEST OF 1 LEMON

MINCED ZEST OF 1 LIME

MINCED ZEST OF 1 ORANGE

½ CUP FINELY CHOPPED MIXED HERBS SUCH AS CHIVES, TARRAGON, AND FLAT-LEAF PARSLEY

¼ CUP CRÈME FRAÎCHE, WHIPPED

2 TABLESPOONS CHOPPED LEMON CONFIT (*page 258*)

Cut a piece of cheesecloth large enough to wrap the fillet. Mix the sugar with the salt. Spread 1 cup of the sugar mixture on the cheesecloth. Lay the fillet, skin side down, on the sugar mixture, then sprinkle it with another cup of the sugar and salt. Mix the fennel with the parsley, chervil, tarragon, coriander, fennel, pepper, and the zests. Scatter the fennel mixture evenly over the fish. Top with the remaining sugar mixture. Wrap the cloth around the fish, then place it on a plate. Place another plate on top of the fish and cure it in the refrigerator for 24 hours, pouring off any liquid that accumulates. Turn the fillet over and cure for 24 hours more.

Brush off the cure, then rinse and dry the fish. Top the fillet with the mixed herbs. Thinly slice the char and serve accompanied by whipped crème fraîche and chopped lemon confit.

Pickled sardines

MARCO CANORA'S MOTHER, LAURA, *is famous for the cooking seminars she leads in Tuscany. A local woman named Carlotta used to lend a hand, and would bring along the most delicious pickled anchovies that Marco had ever tasted. He re-created the dish for Craft, instead using sardines, which were more readily available fresh in this country than anchovies.*

Serves 6

1 SMALL FENNEL BULB, CORED AND CUT INTO BATONS (2¹/₂ × ¹/₄-*inch lengths*)

1 SMALL YELLOW ONION, PEELED AND CUT INTO BATONS

1 SMALL CARROT, PEELED AND THINLY SLICED

2 CELERY STALKS, PEELED AND THINLY SLICED

2 TEASPOONS DRIED OREGANO (*Sicilian if available*)

4 BAY LEAVES (*fresh if possible*), TORN OR CHOPPED

KOSHER SALT AND FRESHLY GROUND BLACK PEPPER

9 MEDIUM (*5- to 7-ounce*) SARDINES, FILLETED

2 CUPS CHAMPAGNE VINEGAR

FRUITY EXTRA-VIRGIN OLIVE OIL TO COVER, ABOUT 4 CUPS

Combine the vegetables and place half in a baking dish or bowl large enough to hold the sardines in a single layer. Sprinkle the vegetables with half the oregano and 2 of the bay leaves; season with salt and pepper. Lay the sardines, skin side up, over the vegetables (they should not overlap). Top with the remaining vegetables, herbs, and additional salt and pepper. Pour the vinegar over the sardines. Add 1 cup water. Allow the sardines to cure at room temperature until they are opaque and slightly firm, about 20 to 25 minutes for medium fish.

Pour off the pickling liquid. Cover the sardines and vegetables with olive oil and refrigerate until ready to serve.

Grilled squid

IN THIS RECIPE, *you'll find the peperoncini and Sicilian oregano described in the Chickpea Salad (page 112). Although you could substitute a different hot pepper or standard oregano for these ingredients, these ingredients serve as examples of Craft philosophy about detail: Seemingly small choices have a real effect upon flavor and provide an opportunity to elevate even a simple dish of grilled squid. Be sure to buy fresh squid for this recipe; frozen will turn unpleasantly mushy.*

Serves 6

1¼ CUPS EXTRA-VIRGIN OLIVE OIL

¼ CUP FRESH LEMON JUICE

1 TEASPOON DRIED OREGANO (*Sicilian if available*)

2 DRIED PEPERONCINI, FINELY CHOPPED (*or a large pinch of crushed red pepper flakes*)

2 GARLIC CLOVES, PEELED

KOSHER SALT AND FRESHLY GROUND BLACK PEPPER

3 POUNDS SQUID BODIES AND TENTACLES (*cleaned*)

1 BUNCH FRESH FLAT-LEAF PARSLEY

Light a hot fire in a grill. Combine 1 cup of the olive oil, all the lemon juice, oregano, and peperoncini in a large bowl. Chop the garlic, then add a pinch of salt and continue chopping until it forms a paste. Add the garlic to the marinade and set it aside.

Place 1 tablespoon of the remaining olive oil in another large bowl. Season the tentacles with salt and pepper, then mix with the oil. Grill the tentacles, piling them at the center of the hot grill and turning them over until they begin to char, 7 to 10 minutes. Cut the tentacles in half if large and add them to the marinade while still warm.

Mix the raw squid bodies with the remaining 3 tablespoons of oil. Season generously with salt and pepper, then arrange in a single layer on the grill. Cook just until marked on each side, about 6 minutes in all. When the squid bodies are just cool enough to handle, slice them as thin as possible and add them to the marinade. Allow the marinated squid to cool to room temperature, then cover and refrigerate for at least 2 hours but preferably overnight.

Just before serving, chop the parsley and add it to the squid. Adjust the seasoning if necessary.

Sea urchin with fennel purée

MANY PEOPLE ARE FAMILIAR *with cured sea urchin, called uni, which is widely available in sushi restaurants. For this recipe, however, we use fresh sea urchin in their prickly shells, available by order at a good fish store or Japanese market. (Cured uni tastes vaguely of iodine, and won't work here.) To remove the sea urchin from the shell, insert a scissors into the hole on the flat side. Cut out a large enough circle to insert a demitasse spoon and spoon out the roe.*

Ingredients	*Method*

Purée

2 medium	FENNEL BULBS
about 6 cups	SKIM MILK
1 sprig	FRESH TARRAGON
	KOSHER SALT AND FRESHLY GROUND BLACK PEPPER

FOR THE FENNEL PURÉE

Core then chop the fennel. Put the chopped fennel in a saucepan and cover with skim milk. Add the tarragon and season with salt and pepper. Bring the milk to a simmer over medium heat and cook until the fennel is soft. Purée the fennel in a blender or food processor, adding as much of the cooking liquid as necessary to reach the consistency of very light mashed potatoes. Adjust the seasoning with salt and pepper, strain through a fine sieve, and keep warm over very low heat.

Sea urchin

6 large	SEA URCHINS IN THE SHELL
	KOSHER SALT
	EXTRA VIRGIN-OLIVE OIL
juice of 2	LEMONS
	SEA SALT

Serves 6

FOR THE SEA URCHIN

Remove the roe from the urchins. Gently spoon the urchin innards into a colander. Discard the shells. Fill a very large bowl with cold water. Add enough salt to the water so it tastes briny. Dip the colander or pan into the water and gently shake, allowing the water to clean and very slightly cure the roe.

To serve, place a dollop of warm fennel purée and a piece of roe on small plates. Dress with extra-virgin olive oil, fresh lemon juice, and sea salt.

Roasted sea scallops with scallop jus

SEA SCALLOPS are one of Craft's most popular dishes when in season. Make sure the scallops are perfectly dry before placing them in the pan; this will allow them to brown nicely. For more on scallops, see page 79.

2½ POUNDS LARGE SEA SCALLOPS

2 TABLESPOONS EXTRA-VIRGIN OLIVE OIL

1 SMALL WHITE ONION, PEELED AND CHOPPED

1 SMALL FENNEL BULB, CORED AND CHOPPED

1 CELERY STALK, CHOPPED

KOSHER SALT AND FRESHLY GROUND BLACK PEPPER

¼ CUP DRY WHITE WINE

2 CUPS CHICKEN STOCK

1 SPRIG FRESH TARRAGON, 1 SPRIG FRESH THYME, AND 1 FRESH BAY LEAF TIED IN CHEESECLOTH

3 TABLESPOONS UNSALTED BUTTER

2 TABLESPOONS PEANUT OIL

2 SPRIGS FRESH THYME

Remove the tough muscle at the side of each scallop. Reserve the muscles and set the scallops aside.

Heat the olive oil in a small saucepan over medium heat. Add the onion, fennel, and celery. Season with salt and pepper, and cook, stirring occasionally, until the vegetables are tender but not browned, about 20 minutes. Reduce the heat to medium low. Add the scallop muscles and cook until they are firm, 2 to 3 minutes. Add the wine and simmer until the pan is almost dry, about 7 minutes. Add the stock and the herb bundle. Simmer until the stock has reduced by half. Strain the sauce through a fine sieve, then return it to the pan. Bring the sauce to a simmer over medium

heat. Whisk in 1 tablespoon of the butter. Adjust the seasoning with salt and pepper and keep warm over very low heat.

Dry the scallops with paper towels. Heat a large skillet over medium-high heat. Add the peanut oil. Season the scallops with salt and pepper and add them to the skillet (work in batches if cooking all the scallops at once would crowd the pan). Cook the scallops without moving them until they are golden brown, 1 to 2 minutes, then flip them and add the remaining 2 tablespoons butter and the thyme. Baste with the foaming butter and cook until they are firm outside but just barely warm at the center, about 30 seconds more. Serve the scallops with a drizzle of the sauce.

Scallops

We serve two types of scallops at Craft: small, succulent bay scallops and large sea scallops. The bay scallops we serve come exclusively from Nantucket, where they attach to the eelgrass that grows in the bay. True Nantucket bay scallops are in limited supply, making them hard to get. Often what are sold as bay scallops are actually calico scallops, pencil eraser–sized mollusks without much flavor, harvested off the coast of Florida. True bays are larger—some can be up to an inch in diameter—and abundantly sweet.

Sea scallops, larger and quite meaty, come from Maine. For these we prefer diver scallops—scallops that are hand-harvested by divers who can get into the deep crevices of the ocean floor to find the largest and best specimens that mechanical dredgers miss. At Craft we serve day-boat scallops, brought in the same day they're caught. Since most scallop boats typically stay out on the water for a week or more, day-boat scallops are the freshest (and priciest) available. We eat the round adductor muscle of the scallop—the muscle the scallop uses to open and close its shell. We use the tough connective muscle that joins the scallop to the shell to make sauce, or scallop jus.

Often scallops are dipped in whitening preservative (whiteness in a scallop is not an indication of freshness or quality) or treated with chemicals that cause them to soak up liquid to become heavier. To avoid these problems, make sure to request dry scallops at the fish market, and don't buy any that have been sitting in a pool of liquid. Fresh, untreated scallops may range in color from cream to pinkish gray to pale coral, and may feel sticky. Be sure to dry them again thoroughly before placing in the pan (wet scallops won't brown nicely) and use medium-high heat, so that they sear, rather than sweat.

Pan-roasted soft-shell crabs

SOFT-SHELL CRABS *fly off the menu at Craft as soon as they're in season. I prefer not to dredge the crabs in flour or bread crumbs, seasoning them with just kosher salt and freshly ground black pepper, so you can really taste the delicate crab flavor. The important thing when cooking soft-shells is to not crowd the pan: Even with two pans, you may need to cook the crabs in batches. Simply wipe out the pan after each batch, and repeat the process.*

Serves 6

12 MEDIUM SOFT-SHELL CRABS, CLEANED (*see page 82*)

KOSHER SALT AND FRESHLY GROUND BLACK PEPPER

6 TABLESPOONS PEANUT OIL

6 TABLESPOONS UNSALTED BUTTER

JUICE AND ZEST OF 1½ LEMONS

3 TABLESPOONS CHOPPED CHIVES

Dry the crabs on paper towels. Season 8 of them on both sides with salt and pepper. Heat 2 large skillets over medium-high to high heat. Add 2 tablespoons of the oil to each pan, then add the crabs, top side down. Cook until the crabs sizzle and begin to crisp and brown, 1 to 2 minutes. Turn the crabs and reduce the heat slightly. Add 2 tablespoons of the butter to each pan and cook, basting the crabs with the melting butter, until they are firm,

about 1 minute more. Remove the pans from the heat. Add the juice and zest of half a lemon to each pan. Swirl the lemon butter over the crabs, then drain them on paper towels. Wipe out one of the skillets and repeat cooking the remaining crabs and flavoring with the remaining lemon juice and zest. Serve sprinkled with chives.

How to clean a soft-shell crab

Turn the crab upside down. Peel back the flap with the pointed edge and snip off with sharp kitchen scissors. Turn the crab over. Lift the shell up slightly on the right and left sides to reveal the gills under the shell. Without removing the shell, pull the gills off both edges. Use the kitchen scissors to snip off the mouth and eyes. Pat dry with a paper towel.

Soft-shell crabs

Soft-shell crabs are blue crabs (*Calli-nectes sapidus,* which means "beautiful swimmer") that have recently molted, leaving a soft undershell that usually hardens within hours. To harvest soft-shells at precisely the right moment, most fishermen will put the crabs into pens right before the point of molting, and then fish them out soon after the hard shells are off.

Herein lies the dilemma: The best and most delectable soft-shells are small and very soft. Waiting allows the shells to harden a bit, so that the crabs are less likely to die in transit, but the trade-off is a less tender crab. I tell our purveyors to send the crabs immediately upon molting; I'm willing to take the loss of the ones that don't make it as the price to pay for others that are just right.

The soft-shell season starts around the end of April (in the Carolinas, and then

Maryland) and can go as late as August to early September up in New Jersey. What I love about soft-shells is that they are so accessible and great for eating; you can have the great taste of fresh crab, without the hours of picking labor that go into hard-shell crabs. Soft-shells come raw and lend themselves to a variety of preparations.

When buying, try to find soft-shells that are alive, but as soft as possible. Touch the end of the claws—these are the first to harden, and the softer the point at the end of the claw, the softer (and more palatable) the crab. Since soft-shells are best in spring, I usually like to pair them with spring vegetables—ramps, asparagus, morels, chives—and sauté them lightly, since I think breading and frying the crabs gets in the way of the delicate flavor.

Pan-roasted skate

SKATE IS A FISH *with two big pectoral fins that resemble wings, and this is the part that we eat. It's a wonderfully palatable fish, despite its strange, striated appearance. In the pan, the outside becomes crisp, while the high level of collagen in the flesh melts and leaves the inside creamy and tender. Try to buy thick, meaty fillets; they will be the most melting of all.*

At Craft, Skate is often served with a flavored butter, like the ramp butter (see page 260). If ramps are not available, leeks or chives will also work. Capers are also a good choice—the salt and astringency makes a nice counterpoint to the creaminess of the fish.

Serves 6

ABOUT ¾ CUP SUPER-FINELY GROUND FLOUR (*Wondra*)

KOSHER SALT AND FRESHLY GROUND BLACK PEPPER

6 6-OUNCE SKATE WINGS

4 TABLESPOONS PEANUT OIL

4 TABLESPOONS UNSALTED BUTTER

4 SPRIGS FRESH THYME

RAMP BUTTER (*page 260*) (*optional*)

Mix the flour with a little salt and pepper. Dip the ridged side of each of the skate wings in the flour mixture. Shake off the excess. Salt and pepper but do not flour the second sides.

Heat 2 large skillets over high heat (alternatively, work in batches). Add 2 tablespoons of the oil to each pan, then add the skate wings, floured side down. Cook the skate until the first sides begin to brown, about 3 minutes. Turn the skate and reduce the heat to medium. Add half of the butter and thyme to each pan and continue cooking, basting the skate with melting butter, until the fish is opaque and tender throughout, 2 to 3 more minutes.

Roasted cod

COD IS MILD *and meaty, so it pairs nicely with the tangy acidity of a sauce like salsa verde. This recipe will also work with other thin-skinned, hearty fish, like black sea bass. For more on cod, see page 87.*

Serves 6

4 TABLESPOONS PEANUT OIL

KOSHER SALT AND FRESHLY GROUND BLACK PEPPER

6 1¼-INCH-THICK, 7¼-OUNCE SKIN-ON COD

4 TABLESPOONS UNSALTED BUTTER

2 SPRIGS FRESH THYME

ABOUT 1¼ CUPS SALSA VERDE, *(page 264) (optional)*

Warm 2 large skillets over medium-high heat. Add 2 tablespoons of the oil to each. Salt and pepper the fish fillets and place three, skin side down, in each pan. Pan-roast the fish until the skin is crisp and the flesh opaque about a fourth of the way up each fillet, about 7 minutes. Turn the fish fillets over and reduce the heat to medium. Add half the butter and thyme to each skillet and cook, basting the fish with the melting butter. Cook cod (which is best cooked through) about 5 minutes more, and salmon (which is nice medium-rare) about 3 minutes more. (The fish can alternatively be cooked in batches, wiping the pan clean in between.) Serve with salsa verde, if desired.

Cod

Cod was once the most plentiful fish in the North Atlantic—a cornerstone of the Cape Cod economy, and a staple for inexpensive food like fish-and-chips and cod cakes. All that changed with the advent of factory trawlers, which decimated cod stocks and led to the closure of Georges Bank, one of the world's largest fishing grounds. In the years I've been cooking, I've watched the price of cod increase about sevenfold.

At Craft I like to buy Chatham Bay cod, from the Cape, because the port's proximity to Chatham Bay guarantees us a steady supply of day-boat fish—fish caught and shipped out the very same day. (Expensive but worth it.) Also, Chatham Bay cod are still caught using the traditional rod-and-reel method, which minimizes stress and improper handling of the fish. These may seem like minor distinctions, but the difference is noticeable on the palate and crucial to me as a chef.

Cod is a good, meaty, mild white fish that appeals to almost everyone. On Christmas eve, my family eats *baccala*—salt cod—as part of our big Italian seafood meal. This year I also baked large cod fillets with a sprinkling of breadcrumbs, garlic, and parsley over the top, and even the kids were asking for seconds. Fillets are usually sold skinless, so I recommend calling your fishmonger ahead of time to order skin-on cod. The skin helps keep the fish from flaking apart when cooking.

Sturgeon wrapped in prosciutto

"LARDING" FILLETS in this manner works well with a variety of fish; you could easily substitute striped bass or red snapper. I recommend going with whatever is freshest. Prosciutto is a leaner wrapper than bacon and adds a nice salty flavor to the fish without too much fat. Prosciutto also stays flat while it cooks, making for a nice presentation.

Serves 6

6 1½-INCH-THICK, 7-OUNCE
STURGEON FILLETS

KOSHER SALT AND FRESHLY
GROUND BLACK PEPPER

ABOUT ⅓ POUND PROSCIUTTO
(paper-thin slices)

4 TABLESPOONS PEANUT OIL

4 TABLESPOONS UNSALTED BUTTER

2 SPRIGS FRESH THYME

Heat the oven to 400°F. Season each of the fillets with salt and pepper. Wrap two pieces of prosciutto, slightly overlapping, around the center of each fillet (the prosciutto will not cover the ends of the fish).

Heat 2 large ovenproof skillets over medium high. Divide the oil between the skillets. Add 3 fillets to each pan, and cook until the pans are once again hot, 1 minute or so. Reduce the heat to medium and cook the fillets until the first sides are crisp, about 1 minute. Flip each fillet and cook the second sides until they, too, are lightly browned, 1 to 2 minutes. Roll each fillet onto its side. Add half the butter and thyme to each pan. Cook, basting the fish with butter, until the third sides are also caramelized, another 1½ minutes or so. Rotate the fish once more and cook the final sides, basting frequently. (Cooked for a total of 6 minutes, the fish will be a little translucent at the center; reduce the heat and cook the fish longer for more well-done.) Slice and serve.

Lunch Service

Thursday, May 16

"PICK UP! Short ribs! Gnocchi! Chard!"

James Tracy, lunch sous-chef, tears another white square from the small printer that jerks and spits out orders with the insistent thrust of tickertape.

"Short ribs!" "Gnocchi!" "Chard!" comes the echo from various points on the line as cooks confirm and dip into cooler drawers, with their stocks of prepped ingredients. They respond to each new order with a concise correlating action. Food is placed into pans, the cooks turning, swiveling, pressing fingers into fillets to gauge heat and doneness, moving pots from one burner to another, from burner to oven and back again. Spoonfuls of potato purée, pillowy and steaming, are ladled into a miniature copper pot and handed down the line. Roasted mushrooms are tumbled into a platter, and handed off. Everything is motion; there is no time to pause or to reflect, merely to cook, to taste, to test, to pass it on.

A fish cook calls out, "I need plates," his eyes fixed on the eight burners and six sauté pans that make up his domain. Immediately a porter appears

behind him, balancing a white tower of plates, hips swiveling to avoid the back-and-forth of shoulders, fingers, halibut, peas from cooler into pan. It is a delicate pas de deux of less-than-delicate guys that miraculously deposits the plates where they need to be and the porter back where he began, empty-handed. "Thanks!" the cook tosses over his shoulder, but the porter is already gone.

"Ramps!" ("Ramps!")
"Scallops!" ("Scallops!")
"Skate!" ("Skate!")

At the pass, runners stand at attention, wiping errant drips from the edges of plates, before hoisting heavy trays of food and turning on their heels in one improbable swoop. A few more steps and they will be on the stairs, leaving the heat and noise and entering a place of genteel murmurs and the clink of glasses, a universe away from the boisterous kitchen. But down below, at the pass, James crouches over a platter, spooning ramp butter over skate before tearing the next sheet from the printer and starting again.

"Monkfish!" ("Monk!")
"Peas!" ("Peas!")
"Lobster!"
And so on.

Beurre fondue

INGREDIENT PORTRAIT

Beurre fondue is a simple sauce made by whisking melting butter into water to form a light, creamy emulsion. The cooks at Craft and I keep a small container of it on hand (usually in a bain-marie by the stove, to keep it from cooling and breaking down) that we dip into throughout the night to baste fish or meats or to make a base for vegetables as they come up to temperature. You'll find we've used beurre fondue periodically throughout the book, usually as a braising liquid for dishes like Braised Lobster (page 93) and Braised Morels (page 154). In both instances, as the main ingredient cooks it releases its own juices into the beurre fondue, thinning it and creating a simple and flavorful sauce that can be spooned over the finished dish. Beurre fondue is also the perfect medium in which to heat and serve homemade Gnocchi, page 172.

Lobster braised in beurre fondue

THIS RECIPE *takes a lot of work but makes a great dinner-party dish. First, most of the hard work is done in advance (blanching the lobster and making the stock). Second, the cooked lobster can rest for up to 20 minutes in the beurre fondue before serving, giving you an ample window in which to work on other things.*

Serves 6

6 1½-POUND LIVE LOBSTERS

2 TABLESPOONS PEANUT OIL

1 SMALL WHITE ONION, PEELED AND CHOPPED

1 SMALL FENNEL BULB, CORED AND CHOPPED

2 SMALL CELERY STALKS, CHOPPED

KOSHER SALT AND FRESHLY GROUND BLACK PEPPER

1 TEASPOON TOMATO PASTE

4 SPRIGS FRESH THYME

1 BUNCH FRESH TARRAGON

2 ROASTED GARLIC CLOVES (*page 260*), PEELED

1 POUND UNSALTED BUTTER, CHILLED AND CUT INTO SMALL PIECES

Heat the oven to 350°F.

Prepare the lobster by separating the tails and claws from the bodies. Split the bodies in half with a sharp knife. Blanch the tails and claws in boiling salted water, cooking the tails for 1 minute and the claws for 3. Refresh the tails and claws in ice water, then wrap in plastic and refrigerate.

Meanwhile, heat the oven to 350°F. and make the stock. Rinse the lobster bodies and remove all the soft matter including the gills (reserve the roe, if any, for flavor

ing sauces). Place the oil and the lobster bodies in a pan and roast in the oven until the lobster shells begin to redden, about 20 minutes. Add the onion, fennel, and celery. Season with salt and pepper and tomato paste and roast until the vegetables start to brown, about 45 minutes longer. Transfer the roasted lobster shells and vegetables to a large pot. Add the thyme, half of the tarragon, and water to cover, about 6 quarts. Simmer until the stock has reduced by about half, 1½ to 2 hours. Strain the stock through a fine sieve. Ladle 2 cups of the stock into a

(Continued)

small saucepan (refrigerate or freeze the remaining stock for future use). Reduce the contents of the saucepan by one fourth.

Shortly before serving, remove the meat from the lobster claws and arms. Split the tail lengthwise, exposing the meat but leaving it in the shell.

Combine 1 cup of the reduced lobster stock, the remaining tarragon, and the roasted garlic in a saucepan large enough to hold all of the lobster. Bring the stock to a boil, then reduce the heat to medium-low and gradually whisk in the butter. When all the butter has been incorporated, turn the heat as low as possible and check the temperature with a cooking thermometer. When the thermometer indicates a temperature between 160° and 180°F., add the lobster. Steep the lobster in the warm beurre fondue for at least 15 minutes (it can remain as long as 35 minutes without ill effect).

To make the sauce, heat the remaining lobster stock in another saucepan. Bring it to a boil, then reduce the heat to low. Whisk 4 tablespoons of the beurre fondue into the stock. Season the sauce with salt and pepper. Lift the lobster from the braising liquid with a slotted spoon into serving bowls. Spoon sauce over the lobster and serve.

Braised red snapper

FISH POACHED IN OIL *is an unusual dish, but I like how it leaves the fish moist when it's fully cooked. The vinaigrette introduces flavors of citrus and vinegar and balances out the richness of the oil-poached fish.*

Serves 6

For the vinaigrette

1 CUP FRESH ORANGE JUICE

1 CUP FRESH GRAPEFRUIT JUICE

JUICE OF 1 LEMON

1 TABLESPOON CHAMPAGNE VINEGAR

¾ CUP EXTRA-VIRGIN OLIVE OIL

KOSHER SALT AND FRESHLY GROUND BLACK PEPPER

For the fish

4 TABLESPOONS PEANUT OIL

KOSHER SALT AND FRESHLY GROUND BLACK PEPPER

6 7-OUNCE, SKIN-ON RED SNAPPER FILLETS

ABOUT 4 CUPS EXTRA-VIRGIN OLIVE OIL

1 GARLIC CLOVE, PEELED AND THINLY SLICED

2 SPRIGS OF FRESH ROSEMARY

1 LEMON, THINLY SLICED

For the vinaigrette: Combine the orange, grapefruit, and lemon juices in a saucepan. Bring to a simmer over medium-high heat and reduce to about 2 tablespoons. Combine the reduced citrus juice and vinegar in a bowl. Gradually whisk in the olive oil. Season the vinaigrette with salt and pepper and set aside.

For the snapper: Heat 2 large skillets over medium-high heat. Divide the peanut oil between the pans. Salt and pepper the snapper and add the fillets, skin side down, to the skillets. Cook until the skins crisp, about 3 minutes, then remove the fish from the pans. Wipe out one of the skillets. Fit the fish, skin side up, into the clean skillet (the fillets should fit snugly). Add enough olive oil to come about three quarters of the way up the fish fillets. Add the garlic, rosemary, and lemon and warm over medium heat. When the first bubbles appear, lower the heat. Cook over low (the oil shouldn't bubble at all) until the fish is tender and opaque, about 7 minutes. Drain the fish on paper towels, then serve with the vinaigrette.

Braised monkfish

CRAFT'S EXECUTIVE CHEF, *Marco Canora, modeled this dish on cacciucco, a classic stew from Viareggio, one of the only seaside towns in Tuscany. When Marco was chef at the Tuscany Inn on Martha's Vineyard, that fish stew was his biggest seller, but he couldn't see how a stew would translate to our "single ingredient" concept at Craft. Finally he decided to marry the flavors of a cacciucco to one fish, in order to create a more elemental dish, and he chose monkfish on the bone, which lends itself so well to braising because of its richness and firm texture. His idea was good; the braised monkfish has consistently been one of our best-sellers at Craft.*

Serves 6

2 CUPS BLONDE SOFFRITTO BASE (*made with fennel in place of carrot if possible; page 255*)

2 TABLESPOONS DRIED OREGANO (*sicilian if available*)

½ TEASPOON CHOPPED PEPERONCINI (*or a pinch of crushed red pepper*)

7 CUPS CANNED TOMATOES WITH THEIR JUICES, PURÉED

1½ CUPS WHITE WINE

1½ CUPS VEAL STOCK (*page 252*), OR STRONG BROWN CHICKEN STOCK (*page 251*)

¾ CUP FUMET (*page 253*)

BONES AND HEAD FROM 1 BASS OR OTHER LEAN WHITE-FLESHED FISH (*optional*)

1 SPRIG FRESH ROSEMARY, 1 SPRIG FRESH THYME, AND 1 BAY LEAF, TIED IN CHEESECLOTH

KOSHER SALT AND FRESHLY GROUND BLACK PEPPER

6 8-OUNCE, BONE-IN OR 6 6-OUNCE BONELESS PIECES OF MONKFISH

2 TABLESPOONS EXTRA-VIRGIN OLIVE OIL

MINCED ZEST OF 1 LEMON

1 MEDIUM TOMATO, SEEDED AND CUT IN SMALL DICE

Place the soffritto, oregano, and peperoncini in a large high-sided skillet. Heat over medium and cook until the soffritto is amber, about 20 minutes. Add the puréed tomatoes and simmer, stirring frequently, until the oil begins to separate, about 25 minutes. Transfer ½ cup of the soffritto to a bowl and reserve. Add the wine to the soffritto remaining in the pan. Simmer until the soffritto no longer tastes or smells like wine, about 15 minutes. Add the veal stock and fumet fish head and bones (if using), and herb bundle. Season with salt and pepper and gently simmer over medium heat until the braising mixture has reduced by half, about 1 hour. Discard the fish head, bones, and herb bundle. Adjust the seasoning and keep warm over low heat.

Heat the oven to 350°F. Dry the monkfish with paper towels. Heat a large ovenproof skillet over medium heat. Add the olive oil. Season the fish on both sides with salt and pepper. Brown the fish on one side, about 7 minutes. Turn the fish, then ladle the braising mixture over it. Transfer the skillet to the oven. Oven-braise uncovered for 20 minutes.

Combine the reserved soffritto with the lemon zest and diced tomato. Spoon the mixture over the fish. Continue oven-braising, basting occasionally, until the fish is tender and cooked through (the fish should be opaque and hot at the center—check by inserting a metal skewer), about 20 minutes longer. Serve immediately.

Braised striped bass

IN THIS RECIPE *striped bass is braised in an aromatic broth, which lends its flavors to the fish and keeps it moist throughout the cooking process. Since this broth turns cloudy as the fish cooks, I reserve a small amount for serving over the fish later. At the restaurant we add fresh onion, carrot, celery, and fennel that are blanched or sweated specifically for this purpose. Here we simplify, and garnish with a sprig of fresh thyme.*

Serves 6

For the broth

3 TABLESPOONS EXTRA-VIRGIN OLIVE OIL

½ YELLOW ONION, PEELED AND SLICED

1 SMALL CARROT, PEELED AND SLICED

½ FENNEL BULB, CORED AND SLICED

1 CELERY STALK, SLICED

1 SHALLOT, PEELED AND SLICED

KOSHER SALT AND FRESHLY GROUND BLACK PEPPER

1 TEASPOON CORIANDER SEEDS, TOASTED

1 TEASPOON FENNEL SEEDS, TOASTED

1 CUP DRY WHITE WINE

1 CUP WHITE WINE VINEGAR

1 QUART FUMET (*page 251*)

3 SPRIGS FRESH THYME

1 BAY LEAF

3 SPRIGS FRESH TARRAGON

1 SPRIG FRESH ROSEMARY

For the bass

4 TABLESPOONS EXTRA-VIRGIN OLIVE OIL

KOSHER SALT AND FRESHLY GROUND BLACK PEPPER

6 6-OUNCE, SKIN-ON STRIPED BASS FILLETS (*about 1¼ inches thick*)

3 SPRIGS FRESH THYME, PLUS ADDITIONAL FOR GARNISH IF DESIRED

For the broth: Heat the olive oil in a large pot over medium heat. Add the onion, carrot, fennel, celery, and shallot and season with salt and pepper. Sweat the vegetables until they are soft, about 20 minutes. Add the coriander and fennel seeds, wine, and vinegar and simmer until reduced by half, about 10 minutes. Add the fumet, 1 cup water, the thyme, bay leaf, tarragon, and rosemary. Simmer until the flavors in the broth blend, about 15 minutes; set aside to cool.

For the bass: Divide the oil between 2 large skillets and heat over medium. Salt and pepper the fish and add it, skin side down, to the skillet. Add the thyme and cook until the skin is crisp, about 6 minutes. Turn the fish, then ladle 2 cups of the broth with vegetables into each skillet,

reserving the remainder. Bring the broth to a simmer, then reduce the heat to medium-low and gently simmer the bass until it is opaque throughout, about 5 minutes more.

To serve, bring the reserved broth to a simmer, then ladle it into warm shallow bowls. Place a piece of fish in each bowl, garnish with fresh thyme, if desired, and serve.

Striped bass

I love this fish. Love to catch it, love to eat it. By law, stripers must be a full 28 to 34 inches to be kept, depending upon the state in which they're caught, which makes them a great restaurant fish; their size allows us to cut nice, thick fillets that are great for roasting. (The thicker the fillets, the longer it has to develop nice roasted flavors without overcooking.) There is some precision involved in cooking striped bass perfectly. I don't believe in cooking it to death, but I don't serve it rare in the center, either. The fillet should be *just* cooked through—a matter of only a few seconds here separates that ideal from over- or undercooked—but the little bit of time really makes a difference in both flavor and texture. In the kitchen at Craft, you'll see my cooks touching the fillets frequently as they roast in the pan; I feel this is the only way to determine if fish is cooked exactly right. You should do the same, touching the fish early to see what undercooked feels like, and then again throughout, noticing as the fillet begins to firm in the center and lose some of its "give." Unless you like your fish very well done, I recommend removing it from the heat before it gets very firm to the touch. In fact, you should always remove fish when it still feels a trifle undercooked as it will continue to cook for a short time on its own.

Fifteen years ago stripers were pretty much gone. They had been overfished by both commercial and sport fishermen— and since no limits to either existed, striped bass were on the brink of extinction. About twenty years ago, PCB levels in local waterways rose dramatically (mostly due to the dumping of industrial waste into the Hudson River and the Chesapeake Bay), making the fish from those waters unfit to sell. Commercial striped bass fishing collapsed, stripers were left alone to propagate, and the stocks naturally came back. As a result of lawsuits, PCBs were cleaned up about seven or eight years ago, only this time, when commercial fishing resumed, it was subject to strict limits. Now, happily, stripers are once again in such abundance that these limits have finally been loosened. On the North Atlantic coast, the fishing season lasts from about May to October, a nice, long season, which makes striped bass a wonderful, dependable fish for the restaurant.

For more information about fishing and environmental safety, go to www.riverkeeper.org.

vegetables

Salads

Mixed lettuces 104
with house vinaigrette

Herb salad 106

Beet salad 109
with beet vinaigrette

Shaved fennel salad 110

Celery root remoulade 111

Chickpea salad 112

Leek salad 114

Roasted

Pan-roasted ramps 117

Roasted spring onions 118

Pan-roasted asparagus 119

Roasted beets 120

Pan-roasted cauliflower 121

Roasted Jerusalem
artichokes 124

Roasted carrots 126

Sautéed

Sautéed sugar snap peas 127

Sautéed lamb's quarters 128

Sautéed broccoli rabe 129

Sautéed swiss chard 130

Sautéed spinach 132

Braised

Braised ramps 133

Braised spring peas 134

Braised endive 135

Braised salsify 137

Braised baby fennel 138

Braised carrots 139

Creamless cream corn 141

Braised cardoons 142

Puréed

Puréed parsnips 143

Butternut squash purée 146

Celery root purée 147

Mixed lettuces with house vinaigrette

I'VE CHOSEN TO BE *deliberately vague here on which greens to use, since I would like you to choose based on what is fresh and looks delicious to you at the market. Choose whole heads of tender young lettuces, rather than precut, prewashed varieties, and go for the juiciest leaves at the center. When dressing the salad, use less vinaigrette than you think you'll need— we recommend you start with 1/4 cup—and taste, adding more only if necessary. The amount of dressing you use will vary based on the size of the heads and the type of lettuce (the most delicate varieties need less). For more on salad greens, also known as mesclun, see page 107.*

Serves 6

LEAVES FROM 2 MEDIUM OR
3 SMALL HEADS OF LETTUCE,
WASHED AND TORN

KOSHER SALT AND FRESHLY
GROUND BLACK PEPPER

ABOUT 1 CUP HOUSE VINAIGRETTE
(*page 265*)

Season the lettuce with salt and pepper.
Lightly dress the salad with vinaigrette,
then arrange on plates.

Herb salad

AT CRAFT WE OFTEN *use soft herb leaves as a small side salad alongside roasted or marinated fish; the clean, light herb notes play up just about anything. Add the lemon juice and olive oil sparingly, tasting as you go, since the herbs can be overwhelmed by too much dressing. To wash fresh herbs, rinse under a thin stream of tap water, or dip them into a bowl of cool, standing water and lift out. Shake to remove excess water, and dry gently on paper towels before dressing.*

Serves 6

2 CUPS MIXED SOFT HERB LEAVES SUCH AS FLAT-LEAF PARSLEY, BASIL, TARRAGON, CHIVES, CHERVIL, AND MINT

1 CUP CLEANED FRISÉE

KOSHER SALT AND FRESHLY GROUND BLACK PEPPER

1 TABLESPOON FRESH LEMON JUICE

3 TABLESPOONS EXTRA-VIRGIN OLIVE OIL

Season the herbs and frisée with salt and pepper. Lightly dress with lemon juice and olive oil. Arrange on plates and serve with cured fish or chilled lobster.

"Mesclun"

There was a time when salad meant a wedge of iceberg—refreshing, but essentially a characterless delivery system for salad dressing and tasty things like croutons and bacon bits. When mesclun first appeared on the scene—that mixture of tiny, carefully picked baby greens—it was a welcome change and a "gourmet" antidote to the blahs of a typical salad. Unfortunately, the beautiful mixtures of baby lettuces that once characterized mesclun have gone the way of most things once they become widely popularized. Today's mesclun—although still made up of small leaves—has become a mixture of uninspiring greens that can be prewashed and sold in bulk. To keep up with demand throughout the year, this blend is grown hydroponically or in hothouses (neither of which encourages flavor) and is bred for resilience, to stand up to shipping. When these greens do have any flavor to speak of, it is often overly bitter or harsh and peppery, lacking the nuance and sweetness one would expect from baby greens. Salads made from these greens are less than exciting—a form of filler before or after the main course—and their dressing is more the defining element of the salad than the greens themselves.

I think of lettuces the way I think of tomatoes: The best ones grow in summer. The mass-produced varieties usually look great, but don't taste like much. The sweet, tender lettuces of summer, like heirloom tomatoes, have distinct flavors and characters. They are usually fairly perishable, and the inner leaves—delicate, verdant, and often quite sweet—require little in the way of dressing or adornment, just like the best of the summer tomatoes. I'm not trying to say we should eat salads only in the summer. Thanks to air freight, tender lettuces can be had year-round; but here it becomes especially important to buy entire heads because the outer leaves protect the inner ones, which are prone to bruising. And as the weather cools, heartier varieties like romaine start to make more sense (I'm a great fan of Caesar salad, myself).

At Craft we like to buy whole lettuces and mix them ourselves so that we can control the flavors and textures of what we serve; some of our favorite greens come from Satur Farms out on the North Fork of Long Island (see Resources, page 269). They send us varieties like batavian, summer crisp, lolo rosso, and deer tongue. These greens have so much flavor that they merit their very own category on the menu as an ingredient that can stand alone, not unlike mushrooms or grains. These are the kind of lettuces that are worth tasting, before you dress and are worth dressing sparingly, if at all. I recommend buying whole heads at the green market and going right for the center, where the juiciest and sweetest leaves are waiting. Do this a few times yourself, and you might find yourself walking past that big bin of mesclun in the grocery store once and for all.

Beet salad with beet vinaigrette

If you're buying beets in the green market, try to buy different types along with the classic red—like golden beets, chiogas, and candy stripes. The colors make for an especially striking presentation.

Serves 6

For the salad

24 BABY BEETS

3 TABLESPOONS GRAPESEED OIL

KOSHER SALT AND FRESHLY GROUND BLACK PEPPER

For the vinaigrette

1 CUP PLUS 2 TABLESPOONS EXTRA-VIRGIN OLIVE OIL

1 LARGE SHALLOT, PEELED AND SLICED

¼ CUP RED WINE VINEGAR

¾ TEASPOON DIJON MUSTARD

½ CUP PEELED CHOPPED ROASTED BEETS

KOSHER SALT AND FRESHLY GROUND BLACK PEPPER

For the beets: Heat the oven to 325°F. Trim the green tops and stringy bottoms from the beets. Wash the beets well. Combine the beets and oil in a large bowl. Season with salt and pepper and toss to coat. Line a roasting pan with aluminum foil (this prevents the pan from becoming discolored). Add the beets, cover the pan with more foil, and roast until the beets can be easily pierced with a knife, about 40 minutes. Allow the beets to cool slightly, then carefully peel them. Coarsely chop about 4 of the beets for the vinaigrette; you'll need ½ cup. Set the rest aside to cool.

For the vinaigrette: Heat 2 tablespoons of the oil in a skillet over medium heat. Add the shallot and sweat until it is soft and translucent, about 15 minutes, then transfer to a blender. Add the vinegar, mustard, chopped beets, and salt and pepper. Purée the mixture, then with the blender running gradually add the remaining cup of oil in a steady stream. Adjust the seasoning if necessary with salt and pepper.

Arrange the beets on plates (they may be served whole or halved). Season them with salt, then lightly dress with the vinaigrette.

Shaved fennel salad

FENNEL IS ONE OF *those wonder ingredients that can be used in any of its many forms—bulb, seed, leaf, or frond—depending on the recipe. Fennel can be braised, roasted, or stuffed with meat into sausage casing, but here we simply slice it paper thin and dress it with lemon juice and olive oil. I like to garnish the slices with fennel fronds to add one more layer of delicate licorice to the plate. This salad tastes best right after it is made.*

Serves 6

3 MEDIUM FENNEL BULBS

¼ CUP FRESH LEMON JUICE

½ CUP EXTRA-VIRGIN OLIVE OIL

KOSHER SALT AND FRESHLY GROUND BLACK PEPPER

FENNEL FRONDS, FOR GARNISH (*optional*)

Core the fennel and remove any discolored outer layers. Slice the fennel as thin as possible (this is most easily done with a mandoline). Dress the fennel with lemon juice, olive oil, salt, and pepper. Serve garnished with fennel fronds, if desired.

Celery root remoulade

CELERY ROOT IS NOT *the root of a celery plant, as the name implies. It is its own autumn-harvested root vegetable, also known as celeriac. Celery root has a daunting appearance—twisted, knobby, and usually grimy—but the flesh has a wonderful nutty flavor and is tender enough to eat raw. In this recipe we dress a fine julienne of the root with remoulade, a creamy, mayonnaise-like emulsion that also works well as sauce for cold fish. This recipe yields about 2/3 cup of remoulade, which is probably more than you need, so taste the salad as you dress.*

Serves 6

1 EGG YOLK

1 TABLESPOON PLUS 2 TEASPOONS
FRESH LEMON JUICE

¾ CUP GRAPESEED OIL

KOSHER SALT AND FRESHLY
GROUND BLACK PEPPER

ABOUT 2 POUNDS CELERY ROOT,
PEELED

2 TABLESPOONS FINELY CHOPPED
FRESH FLAT-LEAF PARSLEY

Combine the egg yolk and 2 teaspoons of the lemon juice in a small bowl. Gradually whisk in the oil. Season with salt and pepper.

Slice the celery root as thin as possible (this is best done with a mandoline), then julienne it. Season the celery root with salt, pepper, and the remaining tablespoon of lemon juice. Dress the salad with the remoulade. Add the parsley and adjust the seasoning if necessary.

Chickpea salad

THE PEPERONCINI IN *this dish is a tiny dried hot pepper with a distinctive flavor, which executive chef Marco Canora first came across when he was working at Il Cibrèo, in Florence. Fabio Picchi, the chef, would grab the peppers off the roof of his house, where his father laid them out to dry. Picchi also introduced Marco to dried Sicilian oregano, grown only in the shade, which is even more aromatic and pungent than other varieties. Any importer of Italian ingredients should have it, or be able to order it for you. (See Resources, page 269.) Plan ahead for this salad. Although the recipe is simple, the chickpeas must marinate overnight.*

Serves 6 to 8

For the chickpeas

3 CUPS DRIED CHICKPEAS (*about 1 pound*), SOAKED OVERNIGHT

2 TABLESPOONS EXTRA-VIRGIN OLIVE OIL

1 YELLOW ONION, PEELED AND QUARTERED

1 CELERY STALK, HALVED

2 MEDIUM CARROTS, PEELED AND HALVED

4 SPRIGS FRESH ROSEMARY AND 4 SPRIGS FRESH THYME TIED IN CHEESECLOTH

KOSHER SALT AND FRESHLY GROUND BLACK PEPPER

For the marinade

1 CUP SMALL DICE OF RED ONION

1 CUP RED WINE VINEGAR

1 CUP SMALL DICE OF CELERY

1 LEMON

2 LARGE SPRIGS FRESH ROSEMARY

2 GARLIC CLOVES, CRUSHED AND PEELED

1 TABLESPOON DRIED OREGANO (*Sicilian if available*)

½ TEASPOON CHOPPED PEPERONCINI (*or crushed red pepper to taste*)

ABOUT 3 CUPS EXTRA-VIRGIN OLIVE OIL

KOSHER SALT AND FRESHLY GROUND BLACK PEPPER

1 CUP FINELY CHOPPED FRESH FLAT-LEAF PARSLEY

For the chickpeas: Drain the chickpeas. Heat the oil in a large pot over medium heat. Add the quartered onion, celery, and carrots and cook, stirring occasionally, until the vegetables begin to color, about 15 minutes. Add the herb bundle and chickpeas and mix with the vegetables. Add water to cover by 2 inches and bring to a gentle simmer. Reduce the heat to medium-low, season with salt and pepper, and cook with just an occasional bubble until the chickpeas are soft, about 1½ hours. Remove the pot from the heat and allow the chickpeas to cool for about 15 minutes.

For the marinade: Meanwhile, combine the red onion and red wine vinegar in a small bowl and set aside for 15 minutes.

Drain the onion and combine it with the diced celery in a large bowl. Peel the lemon, cut away the pith, then julienne the rind. Juice the lemon and refrigerate. Add the rind to the bowl. Add the rosemary, garlic, oregano, peperoncini, and 1 cup of the olive oil. Drain the warm chickpeas and add them to the marinade. Season with salt and pepper and add enough additional oil so the chickpeas are fully covered. Cover the bowl with plastic wrap and refrigerate overnight.

To serve, allow the salad to come to room temperature. Lift the chickpeas out of the marinade with a slotted spoon. Add the chopped parsley, lemon juice, and salt and pepper to taste.

Leek salad

THERE IS A HIDDEN *gem deep inside every leek, just above the white part, right where the leek begins to go green. Right there, hidden at the core, is the most tender part—a delicate whitish green—that feels like the heart of the vegetable. It is this "heart" that should be sliced thin and blanched quickly at the end of the recipe. This will impart a slight grassy kick to the deeper onion flavors of the braised leeks and the puréed leek vinaigrette that forms the base of the dish.*

Serves 6

For the braised leeks

9 LEEKS

1 BUNCH FRESH THYME

KOSHER SALT AND FRESHLY GROUND BLACK PEPPER

MINCED ZEST OF 1 LEMON

2 BAY LEAVES, CRUMBLED

1 CUP DRY WHITE WINE

For the dressing

¾ CUP EXTRA-VIRGIN OLIVE OIL

1 LEEK, WHITE PART ONLY, CHOPPED

KOSHER SALT AND FRESHLY GROUND BLACK PEPPER

½ TEASPOON DIJON MUSTARD

2 TABLESPOONS PLUS 1 TEASPOON CHAMPAGNE VINEGAR

1 TABLESPOON CHOPPED FRESH CHERVIL

FLEUR DE SEL

For the leeks: Heat the oven to 350°F. Pull off the tough or torn outer layers of the 9 leeks to be braised. Cut off the top green portion and the bottom strings but leave the root end intact. (The trimmed leeks should be white or pale green and 3 to 4 inches long.) Set aside 3 of the dark green leek tops and discard the remaining trimmings. Split the trimmed leeks lengthwise.

Wash the leeks, allowing water to run between the leaves but holding the leeks in one piece. Scatter the thyme over the bottom of a flame-proof baking dish large enough to hold the leeks in a single layer. Lay the leeks over the thyme, cut side up. Season the leeks with salt and pepper, then sprinkle with the lemon zest and bay leaves. Add the wine and enough water to

(Continued)

barely cover the leeks. Cover with aluminum foil, then bring to a simmer over medium-high heat. Transfer the leeks to the oven and braise until they are tender, about 30 minutes. Remove the leeks from the oven. Cool in the braising liquid uncovered. Cover and chill (still in the liquid).

For the dressing: Heat 2 tablespoons of the oil in a medium skillet over medium-low heat. Add the chopped leek, salt, and pepper and sweat, stirring frequently, until the leeks are soft, about 15 minutes. Transfer the sweated leeks to a blender. Add the mustard, 2 tablespoons of the vinegar, and salt and pepper and purée.

With the motor running, gradually add ½ cup of the oil. Adjust the seasoning with salt and pepper and stir in the chervil.

Thinly slice the inner cores of the reserved leek tops (discard the tough outer leaves). Blanch the sliced leeks for 1 to 2 minutes—they should still be a little crisp. Refresh the leeks in ice water, then drain.

To serve, dress the sliced leeks with the remaining vinegar and olive oil. Season them with fleur de sel. Spoon the vinaigrette onto plates. Arrange the braised leeks on the vinaigrette, then top with the sliced leeks.

Pan-roasted ramps

RAMPS ARE WILD LEEKS *that appear fleetingly in early spring. They offer up a subtle garlic flavor — easier to integrate into most dishes than regular garlic—along with a hint of delicate onion. Aside from their great flavor, ramps are also versatile and work well within the "waste nothing" mentality of a busy restaurant. We slice the long tops ribbon-thin (a chiffonade) and use them as a garnish for this dish, or for Braised Ramps (page 133). In fact, for the short period of time that they're available, we recommend using ramps wherever you would ordinarily reach for shallots or garlic—in place of garlic in pasta with olive oil, for example, or in place of shallots in an oyster mignonette.*

Serves 6

2 POUNDS YOUNG RAMPS

2 TO 3 TABLESPOONS PEANUT OIL

KOSHER SALT AND FRESHLY
GROUND BLACK PEPPER

2 TABLESPOONS UNSALTED
BUTTER

2 SPRIGS FRESH THYME

Trim the ramps by cutting off and discarding the stringy bottoms and separating and reserving the leaves. Wash both the leaves and stems thoroughly. (The leaves can be slivered and used as a garnish or in salads.)

Heat a thin layer of the oil in a large skillet over medium-low heat. Add about half of the ramps (enough to fill but not crowd the pan), season with salt and pepper, then cook until the ramps begin to color,

about 5 minutes. Add half the butter and thyme. Roll the ramps, lightly browning on all sides and cooking until they are tender, about 5 minutes longer, then drain on paper towels. Repeat with the remaining ramps.

To serve, wipe out the pan and heat over medium. Add a skim of oil and all the ramps. Adjust the seasoning with salt and pepper and reheat for 1 to 2 minutes.

Roasted spring onions

WHEN ONIONS ARE *harvested they are pulled out of the ground and left to cure in the sun, where they develop strong flavors and a papery skin. Spring onions, on the other hand, are harvested immediately without being left to cure and are used while still small and sweet. They are a delight to cook with since they have much more sugar than a typical Spanish or red onion, and they have such a subtle onion flavor you could eat them raw. In this recipe, we start by covering the onions and cooking them slowly in herbs and olive oil; the onions give off a sugary liquid that will caramelize beautifully against the natural pattern of the cut vegetable when we finish by pan-roasting them. Choose the smaller spring onions. These have a particularly nice, tender texture.*

Serves 6

18 SMALL TO MEDIUM SPRING ONIONS

KOSHER SALT AND FRESHLY GROUND BLACK PEPPER

6 TABLESPOONS EXTRA-VIRGIN OLIVE OIL

1 SPRIG FRESH ROSEMARY

2 SPRIGS FRESH THYME

3 TABLESPOONS UNSALTED BUTTER

Heat the oven to 300°F. Clean the onions by trimming all but about 1 inch of the green tops. Split the onions lengthwise, then trim the stringy bottoms, leaving just enough of the base to hold each onion together.

Place the onions in a single layer in a large baking pan. Salt and pepper them, then drizzle them with 3 tablespoons of the olive oil. Add the rosemary and thyme to the pan, cover with aluminum foil, and roast until the onions are tender, about 30 minutes.

To serve, divide the remaining 3 table-spoons of oil between 2 large skillets and heat over medium-high. Add the onions in a single layer, cut side down, and cook until they brown, about 5 minutes. Turn the onions. Add the butter and a little more salt and pepper and cook, spooning the butter over the onions, just until they are glazed, about 3 minutes longer.

Pan-roasted asparagus

PENCIL-THIN ASPARAGUS *has become popular, but for roasting I prefer thicker stalks that can cook long enough to develop nice roasted flavors without drying out.*

Serves 6

2 POUNDS MEDIUM ASPARAGUS

2 TO 3 TABLESPOONS PEANUT OIL

KOSHER SALT AND FRESHLY
GROUND BLACK PEPPER

2 TABLESPOONS UNSALTED
BUTTER

2 SPRIGS FRESH THYME

Trim the tough bottoms from the asparagus. Heat a thin layer of oil in a large skillet over medium-low heat. Working in batches, add enough asparagus to fill but not crowd the pan (about half). Salt and pepper the asparagus and cook until they begin to color, about 5 minutes. Add about 1 tablespoon of the butter and a sprig of the thyme. Roll the asparagus in the butter so they brown lightly on all sides and continue cooking until they are tender, about 5 minutes longer. Transfer the cooked asparagus to a plate. Repeat with the remaining asparagus. Just before serving, warm all the asparagus together in the skillet for 1 to 2 minutes.

Roasted beets

FOR PEOPLE WHO *have experienced only boiled or canned beets, the first taste of a roasted beet can be a revelation. Roasting really concentrates the sweetness and earthiness of the vegetable and alters the texture subtly; the beet actually becomes denser, rather than spongy and soft.*

Serves 6

18 MEDIUM BEETS

3 TABLESPOONS GRAPESEED OIL

KOSHER SALT AND FRESHLY GROUND BLACK PEPPER

4 TABLESPOONS EXTRA-VIRGIN OLIVE OIL

Heat the oven to 325°F. Trim the green tops and stringy bottoms from the beets. Wash the beets well.

Combine the beets and grapeseed oil in a large bowl. Season the beets with salt and pepper and toss to coat. Line a roasting pan with aluminum foil (this prevents the pan from becoming discolored). Add the beets, cover the pan with more foil, and roast until the beets can be easily pierced with a knife, about 40 minutes.

Allow the beets to cool slightly, then, while they are still warm, peel them by gently rubbing with a towel. Cut the beets into halves or quarters. Toss them with the extra-virgin olive oil and additional salt and pepper.

Pan-roasted cauliflower

CAULIFLOWER MAY NOT BE CONSIDERED *a very elegant vegetable, but when properly pan-roasted, it makes a deeply satisfying dish—the perfect marriage of vegetable and starch. Although we use only the florets for this dish, see the note below on using the trimmings for cauliflower purée.*

Serves 6

1 HEAD OF CAULIFLOWER (*about 1½ pounds*)

2 TABLESPOONS PEANUT OIL

KOSHER SALT AND FRESHLY GROUND BLACK PEPPER

1 SPRIG FRESH THYME

1 TABLESPOON UNSALTED BUTTER

Trim the cauliflower into small, 1½-inch florets. Reserve the trimmings to make cauliflower purée.

Place the oil in a large skillet and heat over medium-high. Add the florets, salt and pepper, and the thyme. Cook the cauliflower until the florets begin to color, about 7 minutes. Roll the cauliflower in the pan and add the butter. Continue cooking until the cauliflower is just tender and golden, about 5 minutes more. Drain on paper towels, then serve.

Note

The cauliflower trimmings can be used to make purée. Chop the cauliflower and put in a medium saucepan. Cover the cauliflower with milk, season with salt and pepper, and bring to a simmer over medium heat. Cook the cauliflower until it is fully tender, about 20 minutes. Drain the cauliflower, reserving the cooking liquid. Purée the cauliflower in a blender or food processor, gradually adding enough cooking liquid so the purée is the consistency of silky mashed potatoes. Pass the purée through a fine sieve and adjust the seasoning with salt and pepper.

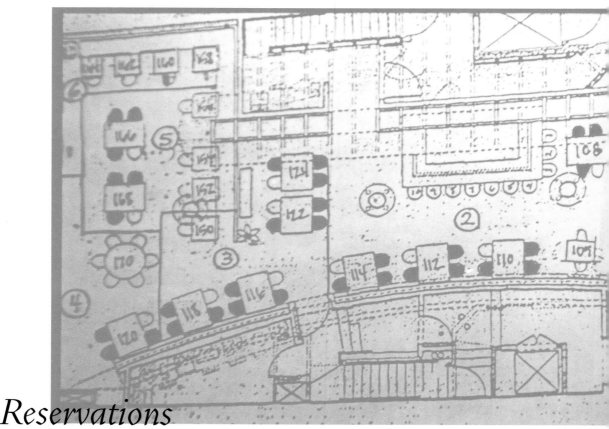

Reservations

Thursday, June 10
2:30 P.M.

IN AN UPSTAIRS OFFICE at Craft eight phone lines are ringing off the hook. A triad of women wearing headsets answer with the standard greeting, "Craft and Craftbar, how can I help you?" and then launch with astounding patience and good humor into the same spiel over and over, answering a variation on the same three questions:

Where are you located?

Is it true I'm going to have to "design" my own food?

Can I book a table for this Saturday at 8 o'clock?

The reservation process is the guest's first portal to the Craft dining experience, and Craft's reservationists—who also function as hosts in the dining room—understand the importance of making a positive impression (despite the inevitable lack of 8 P.M. tables) and drumming up anticipation for the evening even when it is scheduled for weeks, or a month, away. The thinking is that if a guest is impressed with the warmth and hospitality of the person on the phone, he or she will enter Craft with pleasant expectations of the meal to come.

"Everyone's experienced the frustration of a long wait on hold, or a snooty reservationist at a 'hot' new place, at least once in their life," says Tom. "By the time they get to the restaurant, they're already annoyed. Not the vibe we hope to create here."

"Craft and Craftbar, may I ask you to hold?"

"Craft and Craftbar, may I ask you to hold, please?"

"Thank you for holding. You'd like a table for four . . . this Saturday? Eight P.M.? Let me check . . ."

Adwa and Kristen are both pros, easily guiding callers through Craft's menu concept and fielding questions about price, location, and the like. The tricky part comes when the guest asks for a reservation they can't give. "They all want tables between seven and nine P.M.," says Kristen. "Since we can only

grant a few reservations for each hour, those tables go right away." Invariably, she says, guests ask to speak with a manager when they don't get what they want.

Therese, the reservations manager, explains that even if that eight-o'clock table is unavailable, she tries to work with the guest to find a happy alternative. "How about a little earlier, or a bit later? Or a different date when the table is free? How about dining at the bar instead, or next door at Craftbar? I think that's what hospitality is . . . moving forward until we can say 'yes.'" Craft's reservationists purposely pace dinner seating evenly over the hours of 6:00 to 11:00 P.M., in order to keep service flowing smoothly and to keep the kitchen from getting slammed with orders all at once at 8:30 or 9:00 P.M., which would force them to rush food (bad) or make guests wait unduly long for their meals (even worse).

Craft's reservationists have plenty of stories to tell as they juggle the buzzing phone lines, bringing to mind the phone operators from old Hollywood movies, deftly plugging in circuits and getting back to everyone just in the nick of time.

"Lots of people offer us gifts or a 'little extra' if we can fit them in," says Kristen. "Or they'll ask, 'Who do we have to know to get a table?' or 'Is there a special VIP number I can call?'" (There isn't.) People call claiming to be celebrities ("One guy said he was calling on behalf of Tom Cruise, but his caller-ID was, like, in Buffalo") or insist that they are good friends of the owners. "One man called and said he was Tom Colicchio's cousin," says Adwa, "but Tom had never heard of the guy!"

These phone veterans have seen and heard it all. "No, we're Craft *restaurant*," says Kristen calmly into the phone. "Kraft *diner* is on Forty-second Street and Tenth Avenue, sir. But thank you for calling Craft." She hangs up. "I hope they have an eight-o'clock table."

Roasted Jerusalem artichokes

ROASTING JERUSALEM ARTICHOKES *causes them to caramelize and become what executive chef Marco Canora calls "chewy-crispy." When Craft first opened, these and the diver scallops were our most popular items, hands down.*

Serves 6

3 POUNDS JERUSALEM ARTICHOKES

3 TABLESPOONS PEANUT OIL

KOSHER SALT AND FRESHLY GROUND BLACK PEPPER

Heat the oven to 450°F. Scrub the Jerusalem artichokes but do not peel them. Trim them by cutting off any knobs or bumps, then cut each artichoke into rounds (or as close to it as you can get) about 1 inch thick.

Heat the oil in a large ovenproof skillet over high heat. Add the artichokes and cook, stirring just until the skillet is once again hot, about 2 minutes. Salt and pepper the artichokes and transfer the pan to the oven. Roast the artichokes, turning them frequently, until they are tender and brown, 15 to 20 minutes.

Jerusalem artichokes

A Jerusalem artichoke is neither an artichoke, nor from Jerusalem. Actually, it's
the tuberous root of the sunflower plant.
I'm not sure about the artichoke part, but
"Jerusalem" may derive from the Italian
word for sunflower, *girasole*. Jerusalem
artichokes are sometimes known as sun-
chokes and were once used abundantly in
this country, especially in New England. I
love Jerusalem artichokes for their sweet,
delicate flavor and satisfying texture; I
think they make a great alternative to
potatoes, and they can be served in much
the same way, as a hearty accompaniment
to roasted or braised fowl or meat.
Jerusalem artichokes are particularly good
after the first frost, once the vegetable's
starches start to convert to sugar.

Jerusalem artichokes have a dark, knobby
appearance similar to ginger. Choose
firm, unblemished specimens and scrub
well. To prevent the flesh from oxidizing, it
helps to have a bowl of cold water with a
splash of lemon juice at the ready; place
cut pieces in the bowl as you work, and
drain before cooking. When roasted
whole, the center of a Jerusalem artichoke
seems to hollow out, yielding a tiny bit of
soft, sweet inner flesh. At Gramercy Tavern
I'd use this for purée, but it was painstak-
ing work; an entire sheet pan of roasted
Jerusalem artichokes would yield at most a
scant cup. At Craft I prefer to roast a
large dice of the vegetable; the sugars
caramelize and the texture is equal parts
crisp and chewy.

Roasted carrots

FOR THIS DISH *I use baby carrots or Thumbelinas, which are a small, flavorful heirloom variety shaped like a top, but roasting works equally well with mature carrots cut to size. Whichever you choose, I recommend tasting a tip of the raw carrot and using those that have a bright, sweet flavor— these have the highest sugar levels and will caramelize nicely as they cook.*

Serves 6

30 BABY CARROTS (*3 to 4 inches long*)

2 TABLESPOONS PEANUT OIL

KOSHER SALT AND FRESHLY
GROUND BLACK PEPPER

2 TABLESPOONS UNSALTED BUTTER

2 SPRIGS FRESH ROSEMARY

Peel the carrots, then trim them leaving an inch or so of the green top. Heat a large skillet over medium heat. Add the oil, then the carrots. Season with salt and pepper. Cook, rolling the carrots so they color on all sides, until they are golden, about 5 minutes. Add the butter and rosemary and continue cooking until the carrots are tender, about 5 minutes more. Drain the carrots on paper towels before serving.

Sautéed sugar snap peas

Buy sugar snaps *that have taut, shiny skins and that all-important "snap" when bent in two: This translates as high sugar and bright flavor. Make sure to use a pan wide enough to allow the chicken stock to cook off quickly, providing just a light glaze of flavor over the peas before they're finished with butter. Don't worry that this might undercook them; sugar snaps are delicious enough to eat raw, and don't need to cook for much time at all.*

Serves 6

1½ POUNDS SUGAR SNAP PEAS

½ CUP CHICKEN STOCK

KOSHER SALT AND FRESHLY GROUND BLACK PEPPER

3 TABLESPOONS UNSALTED BUTTER

Snap the ends from the peas and pull out the fibrous string that runs the length of the pod. Place the peas in a large high-sided skillet. Add the chicken stock, salt, and pepper and bring to a simmer over medium heat. Cook the peas, turning them in the stock frequently, until the pan is almost dry, about 7 minutes. Add the butter and continue cooking the peas, turning them frequently, until they are tender but still bright green, about 3 minutes more. Adjust the seasoning with salt and pepper.

Sautéed lamb's quarters

LAMB'S QUARTERS *is sometimes called wild spinach, and it grows like a weed, springing up around other vegetables and between the cracks of city sidewalks. The farmers at the green market are amazed that we even want this stuff at Craft, but I like lamb's quarters for its wonderful flavor and body, similar to spinach, but with a lower water content, which makes for a much higher yield after cooking. Lamb's quarters is often grown hydroponically and sold with a small clump of earth attached to the bottom of the bunch: If so, you will need to buy about 6 pounds to get 3 pounds of trimmed greens.*

Serves 6

3 POUNDS TRIMMED LAMB'S
QUARTERS

KOSHER SALT

1 LARGE GARLIC CLOVE, PEELED
AND SLICED

3 TABLESPOONS EXTRA-VIRGIN
OLIVE OIL

FRESHLY GROUND BLACK PEPPER

Wash the lamb's quarters in several changes of water.

Bring a large pot of salted water to a boil over high heat. Plunge the lamb's quarters in the boiling water, then drain as soon as the water returns to a boil. Refresh in ice water, then blot dry with a clean towel.

Combine the garlic and olive oil in a large skillet and warm over low heat. When the garlic begins to color, add the lamb's quarters. Gently warm the leaves in the garlic-infused oil just until heated through, 1 to 3 minutes. Adjust the seasoning with salt and pepper.

Sautéed broccoli rabe

BROCCOLI RABE *is a green from the Cruciferae family, a cousin of mustard greens that resembles broccoli, but with a longer stalk and smaller florets. The slight bitterness of the vegetable is what makes it interesting and a good foil for food that has some sweetness.*

Serves 6

2 BUNCHES BROCCOLI RABE

KOSHER SALT

1 LARGE GARLIC CLOVE, PEELED
AND SLICED

3 TABLESPOONS EXTRA-VIRGIN
OLIVE OIL

FRESHLY GROUND BLACK PEPPER

Trim the broccoli rabe by cutting off the bottom of each bunch and separating the leaves from the flower-topped stems. Snap off and discard the thin stems attached to the leaves. Peel the remaining thick stems, then cut them in half or thirds.

Bring a large pot of salted water to a boil over high heat. Blanch the leaves (plunge them into the boiling water, then remove as soon as the water returns to a boil). Refresh in ice water, then blot dry with a clean towel. Add the stems to the boiling water. Cook until almost tender, about 2 minutes, then drain and refresh in ice water. Dry thoroughly.

Combine the garlic and olive oil in a large skillet and warm over low heat. When the garlic begins to color add both the broccoli rabe leaves and stems. Gently warm the rabe in the garlic-infused oil just until the stems are tender, about 5 minutes. Adjust the seasoning with salt and pepper and serve.

Sautéed swiss chard

THE BIG MISTAKE *people make with chard is cooking the stems and leaves together or—worse—discarding the stems altogether. As you can see in this recipe, we separate the leaves from the meaty stems, blanch them separately (the stems need to cook longer), and then sauté them together quickly for the finished dish. Lately I've seen something called "rainbow chard"—yellow, pink, purple—at the market. The usual red and green varieties have beauty and flavor in abundance, and I recommend you stick with those, as we do at Craft.*

Serves 6

2 POUNDS SWISS CHARD

KOSHER SALT

3 TABLESPOONS EXTRA-VIRGIN OLIVE OIL

1 LARGE GARLIC CLOVE, PEELED AND SLICED

FRESHLY GROUND BLACK PEPPER

Trim any discolored stems or leaves from the chard. Separate the leaves from the stems, then wash both in several changes of water. Cut the stems into 2½-inch pieces.

Bring a large pot of salted water to a boil over high heat. Blanch the leaves (plunge them into the water; remove them with a slotted spoon as soon as the water returns to a boil), refresh them in ice water, then blot dry with a clean towel. Add the stems and cook until they are almost tender, about 3 minutes. Drain the stems, then refresh them in ice water. Set aside with the leaves.

Combine the olive oil and garlic in a large skillet and warm over low heat. When the garlic begins to color add the chard leaves and stems. Warm the chard in the garlic-infused oil just until it is tender, about 5 minutes. Adjust the seasoning with salt and pepper and serve.

Sautéed spinach

SPINACH THROWS *off a lot of water as it cooks. Rather than cooking the spinach until all the water is gone, cook just until tender and then drain gently in a colander or on paper towels for a lighter, fresher taste.*

Serves 6

5 POUNDS FLAT-LEAF SPINACH

3 TABLESPOONS EXTRA-VIRGIN
OLIVE OIL

1 LARGE GARLIC CLOVE, PEELED
AND SLICED

KOSHER SALT AND FRESHLY
GROUND BLACK PEPPER

Trim the spinach stems, then wash the leaves in several changes of water. Blot dry with a clean towel.

Combine the olive oil and garlic in a large skillet and warm over medium heat. When the garlic begins to color add the spinach, a handful at a time. Season the spinach with salt as you go. Cook until the spinach in the pan wilts, then add more. When all the spinach is wilted, cook, stirring occasionally, just until the leaves are thoroughly tender, 1 to 3 minutes more. Drain the spinach, then adjust the seasoning with salt and pepper.

Braised ramps

THE RAMPS IN THIS DISH *are braised in a classic* beurre fondue, *or butter sauce. The braising liquid becomes wonderfully suffused with ramp flavor and makes a great spoon-over sauce for roasted fish. For more on beurre fondue, see page 92.*

Serves 6

2 POUNDS SMALL TO MEDIUM RAMPS

¾ CUP (*1½ sticks*) UNSALTED BUTTER, DICED

KOSHER SALT AND FRESHLY GROUND BLACK PEPPER

Trim the ramps by cutting off and discarding the stringy bottoms and separating and reserving the leaves. Wash both the leaves and stems thoroughly.

Bring ½ inch of water to a simmer in a medium skillet over medium heat. Reduce the heat to medium-low, then whisk in the butter one piece at a time. Add the ramp stems, salt, and pepper to the beurre fondue. Cover and simmer very gently until the ramps are tender, 8 to 12 minutes. Transfer the ramps and some of the braising liquid to serving bowls. Cut the reserved leaves into thin slivers (chiffonade) and arrange on top of the braised ramps.

Braised spring peas

GUESTS AT CRAFT *are thunderstruck by the peas, but the skill here doesn't come so much from the preparation, as from the timing. Peas, like corn, have a small window of time between picking and eating before the high sugar content turns into starch. Most people's experience of peas is of their mild, starchy flavor—pleasant, but not something to write home about. But a spring pea cooked soon after picking is amazingly sweet, with lively, green notes and a great texture. When buying peas, pop one in your mouth. If it's sweet when it's raw, it will be sweet when it's cooked.*

Serves 6

1 LARGE SPRING ONION OR SMALL WHITE ONION, TRIMMED AND PEELED IF NECESSARY

¾ CUP PLUS 2 TABLESPOONS (*1¾ sticks*) UNSALTED BUTTER, DICED

KOSHER SALT AND FRESHLY GROUND BLACK PEPPER

3 CUPS SHELLED PEAS

Cut the onion into a ½-inch dice. Melt 2 tablespoons of the butter in a large skillet over medium-low heat. Add the onion, salt, and pepper and cook, stirring occasionally, until the onion is soft and translucent, about 15 minutes.

Bring a large pot of salted water to a boil. Blanch the peas (plunge them into the water; drain them when it returns to a boil), refresh in cold water, then drain.

Bring ½ inch of water to a simmer in a medium saucepan over medium heat. Reduce the heat to medium-low and whisk in the remaining ¾ cup of butter one piece at a time. Add the peas, onion, salt, and pepper to the beurre fondue and gently braise until the peas are tender, 3 to 5 minutes.

Braised endive

THIS RECIPE INVOLVES *a technique we use again and again at Craft: We start with a mixture of aromatic vegetables, or* mirepoix, *and braise them with the endive in white wine and a bit of vinegar. This technique lends a nice acidity to the dish and imparts a lighter flavor than braising with stock. It can work just as well with other white vegetables, such as artichokes or cardoons (see page 142), but substituting green vegetables here won't work. The acid in the wine will turn them brown.*

Verjus is the juice of unripened grapes. It also offers a pleasing, bright note of acidity without overwhelming the dish with harsh vinegar or citric notes. I recommend keeping a bottle on hand for that purpose. Verjus is readily available in gourmet supermarkets and specialty food shops (see Resources, page 269).

Serves 6

9 BELGIAN ENDIVE

3 TABLESPOONS EXTRA-VIRGIN OLIVE OIL

½ WHITE ONION, PEELED AND SLICED

1 MEDIUM CARROT, PEELED AND SLICED

1 MEDIUM CELERY STALK, PEELED AND SLICED

KOSHER SALT AND FRESHLY GROUND BLACK PEPPER

1 BAY LEAF

1 SPRIG FRESH THYME

¾ CUP WHITE WINE VINEGAR

6 TABLESPOONS DRY WHITE WINE

6 TABLESPOONS VERJUS

Trim the brown ends and any torn or discolored leaves from the endive. Heat the oil in a large, high-sided skillet over medium heat. Add the onion, carrot, celery, and salt and pepper. Cook, stirring occasionally until the vegetables are tender, about 20 minutes. Add the bay leaf, thyme, and endive and stir to coat with oil. Add the vinegar, wine, verjus, and enough water to cover. Season with a little more salt and pepper, then cover first with parchment paper and then with a lid. Simmer over medium-low heat until the endive are tender and can be easily pierced with a knife, about 50 minutes. Discard the bay leaf. Split the endive in half lengthwise and serve in bowls surrounded by braising liquid.

Braised salsify

SALSIFY, A WONDERFUL *autumn vegetable, has a mild, slightly sweet flavor and a starchy texture that makes it a great foil for hearty roasted and braised meats. We use this identical method at the restaurant to cook other tough, fibrous vegetables, like the cardoons on page 142, which require a long cooking time to tenderize; the length of the braise is an opportunity to infuse the vegetable with the tomato and soffritto flavors.*

Serves 6

1 LEMON

2 POUNDS SALSIFY

1 CUP BLONDE SOFFRITTO BASE
(*page 253*)

1 GARLIC CLOVE, PEELED AND
CRUSHED

2 SPRIGS FRESH ROSEMARY

1 TEASPOON TOMATO PASTE

4 WHOLE PEELED PLUM TOMATOES
(*canned or fresh*)

KOSHER SALT AND FRESHLY
GROUND BLACK PEPPER

Squeeze the lemon juice into a large bowl. Add the rinds and 6 cups of water. Peel the salsify, trim the ends, then cut each stalk into lengths about ½ inch thick and 2½ inches long. Place the salsify in the lemon water to keep it from browning.

Heat the soffritto in a large high-sided skillet over medium heat. Add the garlic and rosemary and cook, stirring occasionally, until the garlic is golden and fragrant, about 5 minutes. Add the tomato paste.

Crush the tomatoes and add them with their juices. Season with salt and pepper and cook until the flavors begin to meld, about 10 minutes. Drain the salsify and add it and ½ cup water to the skillet. Cover and simmer over medium-low heat, turning the salsify from time to time, until it is tender, about 45 minutes (adding a little more water if the pan starts to look dry). Adjust the seasoning with salt and pepper and serve.

Braised baby fennel

I PREFER THE FLAVOR *of baby fennel—it has a more concentrated anise flavor than mature fennel—but if you have difficulty finding it, mature fennel can also be substituted; just cut it in half before cooking. Verjus is the juice of unripened grapes; it has a subtle, viniferous acidity and makes a nice alternative to vinegar or cooking wine. Verjus is available in most gourmet shops, but if you can't find it, use more white wine, instead.*

Serves 6

3 TABLESPOONS EXTRA-VIRGIN OLIVE OIL

½ WHITE ONION, PEELED AND SLICED

1 CARROT, PEELED AND SLICED

1 CELERY STALK, SLICED

KOSHER SALT AND FRESHLY GROUND BLACK PEPPER

1 BAY LEAF

1 SPRIG OF FRESH THYME

9 BABY FENNEL, TOPS AND BASES TRIMMED

¾ CUP WHITE WINE VINEGAR

6 TABLESPOONS DRY WHITE WINE

6 TABLESPOONS VERJUS

Heat the oil in a large, high-sided skillet over medium heat. Add the onion, carrot, celery, and salt and pepper. Sweat the vegetables, stirring occasionally, until they are tender, about 20 minutes. Add the bay leaf, thyme, and fennel and stir to coat with oil. Add the vinegar, wine, verjus, and enough water to cover. Season with a little more salt and pepper, then cover and simmer over medium heat until the fennel are tender and can be easily pierced with knife, 30 minutes to 1 hour (depending on the size of the fennel). Discard the bay leaf. Cut the fennel in half lengthwise and serve one and a half per person in bowls surrounded by braising liquid.

Braised carrots

THIS IS AN EXAMPLE *of a fairly mundane ingredient—the humble carrot—elevated by cooking; chicken stock and butter work with the natural sweetness of the carrots and turn them into a standout accompaniment to almost any main course. Covering the skillet with parchment paper allows some steam to escape while keeping the bulk of the braising liquid from evaporating too quickly. At Craft we use Thumbelina carrots, a small heirloom variety shaped like a top that have wonderful, bright flavor. If Thumbelinas are unavailable, baby carrots will work, too.*

Serves 6

30 BABY OR THUMBELINA CARROTS

3 TABLESPOONS UNSALTED BUTTER

ABOUT 2 CUPS CHICKEN STOCK

KOSHER SALT AND FRESHLY GROUND BLACK PEPPER

Peel the carrots, then trim them, leaving an inch or so of green top. Place the carrots and the butter in a high-sided skillet large enough to accommodate the carrots in a snug single layer. Melt the butter over medium-low heat. Add enough chicken stock to just cover the carrots, season with salt and pepper, and cover with parchment paper. Raise the heat to medium and simmer the carrots until they are tender, 10 to 15 minutes. Adjust the seasoning with salt and pepper and serve.

Creamless cream corn

THIS IS MY SON, *Dante's, favorite summer dish at Craft, and it's not hard to figure out why; the white corn, already sweet to begin with, is served in a "cream" derived naturally from puréed corn, further intensifying the corn flavor. Unlike corn on the cob, which is best eaten straight from the field, corn that is a day or two old may work even better here, since some of the natural sugars will have converted to starch, allowing for a thicker cream.*

Serves 6

10 EARS OF WHITE CORN

5 TABLESPOONS UNSALTED BUTTER

1 SMALL YELLOW ONION, PEELED AND DICED

KOSHER SALT AND FRESHLY GROUND BLACK PEPPER

2 TEASPOONS ROUGHLY CHOPPED FRESH TARRAGON

Shuck half the corn and remove the kernels from the husks. Place the corn in a blender and discard the cobs and husks. Purée the corn with ⅓ cup water. Press the purée through a fine sieve and reserve.

Shuck the remaining corn, cut the kernels from the cobs, and reserve. Melt 2 tablespoons of the butter in a large, high-sided skillet over medium heat. Add the onion, salt, and pepper and cook until the onion begins to soften, about 10 minutes. Add the reserved corn, salt, and ½ cup of water. Cook, stirring occasionally, until the corn is almost tender, about 7 minutes.

Meanwhile, transfer the strained corn purée into a double boiler set over barely simmering water. Cook gently, stirring frequently, until the liquid thickens to the consistency of heavy cream, about 3 minutes. Season the purée with salt and pepper. Remove the corn and onion mixture from the heat and stir in the corn cream. Add the tarragon and adjust the seasoning if necessary with salt and pepper.

Braised cardoons

IN UPSTATE NEW YORK, *where executive chef Marco Canora grew up, cardoons grew in his backyard, and he's loved them since he was a kid. Cardoons have a flavor and texture very similar to artichoke hearts, and just like with artichokes, it takes some effort to get to the good part. Start by cutting off the bottom and top of the stalk, and then use a knife or peeler to remove the thick, fibrous ribs on the outside. The innermost part of the stalk is what you're aiming for—sort of like the heart of celery.*

Serves 6

1 LEMON, HALVED

1 BUNCH OF CARDOONS

3 TABLESPOONS EXTRA-VIRGIN OLIVE OIL

½ WHITE ONION, PEELED AND SLICED

1 MEDIUM CARROT, PEELED AND SLICED

1 MEDIUM CELERY STALK, PEELED AND SLICED

KOSHER SALT AND FRESHLY GROUND BLACK PEPPER

1 BAY LEAF

1 SPRIG OF FRESH THYME

¾ CUP WHITE WINE VINEGAR

6 TABLESPOONS DRY WHITE WINE

6 TABLESPOONS VERJUS (*see Resources, page 269*)

Squeeze half the lemon into a large bowl and add 4 cups of water. Peel the cardoons, rub each stalk with the remaining lemon half, then cut it into lengths about 2 inches long and ¼ inch thick. Place the cardoons in the lemon water to prevent browning.

Heat the oil in a large, high-sided skillet over medium heat. Add the onion, carrot, celery, and salt and pepper. Sweat the vegetables, stirring occasionally, until they are tender, about 20 minutes. Add the bay leaf and thyme. Drain the cardoons and add them to the pan; stir to coat with oil. Add the vinegar, wine, verjus, and enough water to cover. Season with a little more salt and pepper, then cover with parchment paper and a lid. Simmer over medium heat until the cardoons are tender, 20 to 30 minutes. Discard the bay leaf. Adjust the seasoning with salt and pepper and serve in bowls surrounded by braising liquid.

Puréed parsnips

PARSNIPS FUNCTION *more like a carrot than a potato here; the vegetable has considerably less starch than a potato, so the purée never risks getting gummy. The sweetness of parsnips makes them a great accompaniment for roasted meats and fish.*

Serves 6

6 MEDIUM TO LARGE PARSNIPS, PEELED AND SLICED

KOSHER SALT AND FRESHLY GROUND BLACK PEPPER

2 TO 3 TABLESPOONS UNSALTED BUTTER (*optional*)

1 TABLESPOON FRESH THYME LEAVES

3 TABLESPOONS EXTRA-VIRGIN OLIVE OIL

Place the parsnips in a large pot. Cover with water. Add a generous amount of salt and bring to a boil over high heat. Cover the pot, reduce the temperature to medium, and cook until the parsnips are tender, about 20 minutes. Using a slotted spoon, transfer the parsnips to a food processor and purée, adding ¾ to 1 cup cooking water to smooth. Season the purée with salt and pepper and press it through a fine strainer. Stir in the butter, if using, then serve the purée topped with thyme and a drizzle of olive oil.

Portrait of a General Manager

October 10
9:35 A.M.

IT'S A DRIZZLY fall morning in an office above Craft. Katie Grieco, Craft's general manager, punches a key on her computer, calling up a log filled with details about the previous evening's service. "The log paints a picture of last night's service for me. It tells me how many guests we served, which regulars came in, anything out of the ordinary that happened." She pauses, eyes scanning the screen. "Last night we did one hundred fifty-five covers, which is low for us. But the weather log shows that it rained, which could explain why." The log also shows that sales were up, especially in wine. "That makes sense on a slow night," Katie explains. "Our captains have a little more time to interact with the table, which makes guests happy. They usually end up trying new things as a result." Katie makes a note in her book. "I'd rather do fewer covers and make more friends, any day."

It may be early, but already Craft's general manager has hired a new electrician and met with a security company to discuss rewiring Craft's security system.

Her weekend was spent relocating Craft's growing squad of reservationists into new offices, moving crates of wine, and plunging (literally) into the finer points of restaurant plumbing. Next she picks up the phone to order a new line of Riedel stemware. "We're upgrading," she explains. "People expect nice glassware if they're going to drink nice wine." Katie chose Riedel because the glasses, with their clean, utilitarian lines, seem to mirror Tom's vision of Craft's overall agenda: quietly unfussy, the best.

11:30 A.M. Therese, the host-reservations manager, pops in to discuss Craft's adoption of Open Table, a computerized reservation system that also builds a guest database. As reservationists and waiters glean personal information—a birthday, a favorite table, a dietary restriction—they enter it into the system. The next time a guest dines at Craft, the staff is clued in to his or her preferences ahead of time. Katie is mildly concerned about the new system's reliability with reservations; there's no margin for error when guests have waited

weeks for a table. They agree to back up the new system with the paper-and-pen method at least until the system is bug-free.

1:00 P.M. An impromptu group—Tom, his assistant Jocelyn, and executive chef Marco—materializes in Katie's office to discuss opening Craftbar for breakfast. Tom is hungry and pushes the idea: "Think about it," he tosses out, "homemade doughnuts, a nice egg *panini* with a little *prosciutto*, good cheese . . ." After some back and forth the busy team decides to shelve the plan, at least for now and concentrate on lunch and dinner. Marco good-naturedly agrees to go downstairs and make the hungry group a few egg *panini* just for the hell of it. Katie follows behind him to check in on lunch service. On the floor she greets a few guests, chats with the lunch manager, and then heads to Craftbar to sample Marco's handiwork.

2:30 P.M. Katie takes a call from a television producer who is scouting locations for an upcoming beer commercial. "Does it matter that we don't serve that

beer at Craft?" she asks the producer. He could care less, he tells her. The company is trying to project "upscale" and is determined to shoot at Craft. Katie is wary, but open. She asks them to fax over a script.

3:30 P.M. Lunch is over and Katie uses the ebb before dinner to gather all of Craft's managers. Front-of-house piles into the office, along with Tom, Marco, Karen from pastry, and their respective sous-chefs in splattered whites. Victor, the service director, discusses ways to make new staff feel welcome, especially waiters, who have gigantic demands of food, service, and wine knowledge placed upon them from their first day. Issues of linen delivery, porters, wine storage, payroll, and scheduling are all handily addressed. Sous-chefs glance at their watches and peel off; dinner's *mise én place* won't wait.

5:20 P.M. As family meal wraps up, Katie straightens a table, lining it up with a row of hanging Edison bulbs that glow against Craft's leather wall.

"My parents used to entertain a lot, and they always included me and my sister, even when we were small. My favorite job was being a hostess, taking people's coats." She laughs, "People still assume I'm a hostess—I guess because I look young—so that hasn't changed." After graduating from Princeton, Katie earned a degree from Cornell University's School of Hotel Administration and then went to work as Tom's assistant at Gramercy Tavern. "I needed to get my foot in the door and I wanted to work somewhere high-end that was friendly, not formal." Tom quickly promoted Katie to manager, sending her for training stints at every department in the restaurant. When he decided to open Craft, Katie followed. Her youth was never an issue for Tom. "The day she walked in the door I could see she was talented, and she represented exactly what I was looking for at Craft. No ego, no posturing, just smart and warm and willing to work hard." Proof came during Craft's first week: The opening—the general man-

ager's equivalent of a triathlon—was on a Wednesday; Katie got married that Saturday. In between she never missed a day.

"I think being a good GM is about keeping cool, treating everyone with a certain amount of care, and listening—to staff, to cooks, to guests. The best part of this job is that every single day I encounter a full spectrum of people—anywhere from recent immigrants to CEOs, aspiring actors to movie stars. It's never dull, and it's never the same two days in a row." Katie looks up as a pair of walk-ins amble through the front door. She quickly steps into position beside a host, glancing at the list on the podium. "We don't have a reservation," one of them says, worried. "That's okay. Welcome." Katie says, giving them a smile. She turns to survey the room, set and at the ready. "Let's see what we can do."

Butternut squash purée

I LIKE TO SERVE *a very silky purée at Craft, which we accomplish by first passing the squash through a food mill and then straining it again through a sieve. A less refined (read: less time-consuming) but equally delicious purée would result from mashing the squash and omitting the straining.*

Serves 6

3 BUTTERNUT SQUASH (*about 10 pounds*), HALVED AND SEEDED

5 TABLESPOONS UNSALTED BUTTER

6 SPRIGS FRESH ROSEMARY

6 SPRIGS FRESH THYME

ABOUT ½ TEASPOON FRESHLY GRATED NUTMEG

KOSHER SALT AND FRESHLY GROUND BLACK PEPPER

2 TABLESPOONS HONEY

Heat the oven to 350°F. Place the squash, cut side up, in a large roasting pan. Divide 3 tablespoons of the butter among the squash halves. Place a sprig each of rosemary and thyme, a pinch of nutmeg, and a generous amount of salt and pepper in each half, then cover the pan with aluminum foil and slowly roast until the squash are very soft, 1½ to 2 hours.

Spoon the squash out of the shells into a food mill (or processor). Purée the squash, then transfer it to a saucepan. Add the honey and the remaining 2 tablespoons of butter. Warm the purée over medium heat, whisking frequently. Adjust the seasoning with salt, pepper, and additional nutmeg if desired. Strain through a fine sieve and serve.

Celery root purée

TO LOOK AT THESE *large, tuberous roots, you'd expect them to make a heavy, thick purée. Surprisingly, celery root purées into a dish that is wonderfully light, airy, and easy on the palate. It's a perfect match with a roasted autumn fish or a light meat like veal.*

Serves 6

3 POUNDS CELERY ROOT, PEELED
AND CUT INTO PIECES

1 CUP SKIM MILK

KOSHER SALT AND FRESHLY
GROUND BLACK PEPPER

6 TABLESPOONS EXTRA-VIRGIN
OLIVE OIL

½ CUP CELERY LEAVES (*optional*)

Combine the celery root and skim milk in a large pot. Add water to cover by about ½ inch. Season generously with salt and bring to a simmer over medium heat. Cook until the celery root is tender, about 30 minutes, then, using a slotted spoon, transfer the celery root to a blender or food processor. Purée the celery root, adding ½ cup of the cooking liquid. Add enough additional cooking liquid so the purée is smooth and light (about ½ cup more). Press the purée through a fine sieve. Adjust the seasoning with salt and pepper and serve dressed with olive oil and garnished with celery leaves, if desired.

mushrooms

Roasted

Pan-roasted hen of the woods
    mushrooms   150

Braised

Braised morels   154
Black truffle   155

Marinated

Marinated lobster
    mushrooms   156
Porcini in parchment   158
Porcini risotto   159

Pan-roasted hen of the woods mushrooms

SINCE CRAFT OPENED, *these mushrooms have developed a true cult following. Hen of the woods take on a lot of flavor due to their curly "tendrils," full of crevices, that crisp up nicely during roasting. We're seeing an increasing array of fresh mushrooms in the marketplace, but if you have difficulty finding hen of thewoods, Marché Aux Delices, our favorite mushroom supplier, can ship them and a wide variety of other fresh, seasonal mushrooms to you overnight (www.auxdelices.com or Resources, page 269). See page 153 for more information on choosing and cleaning mushrooms.*

Serves 6

6 TABLESPOONS EXTRA-VIRGIN OLIVE OIL

3 POUNDS HEN OF THE WOODS MUSHROOMS, TRIMMED AND THICKLY SLICED

KOSHER SALT AND FRESHLY GROUND BLACK PEPPER

2 SHALLOTS, PEELED AND MINCED

2 LARGE GARLIC CLOVES, PEELED AND MINCED

3 TABLESPOONS UNSALTED BUTTER

3 TABLESPOONS FRESH THYME LEAVES

Heat a large skillet over medium heat. Add about 1 tablespoon of oil, then add a large handful of the mushrooms (just enough to loosely cover the bottom of the pan). Salt and pepper the mushrooms and let them sizzle undisturbed until they begin to brown on the bottom, about 2 minutes. Turn each mushroom slice over. Add a little of the minced shallot and garlic and a little butter and thyme. Continue cooking the mushrooms until they are tender, moving them around in the pan from time to time,

about 2 minutes more. Transfer the mushrooms to a plate lined with a paper towel. Wipe out the skillet and repeat until all the mushrooms are cooked.

To serve, wipe out the skillet one last time and heat over medium. Add a skim of oil. Add all the mushrooms, some salt and pepper, and some fresh thyme leaves and butter if you like and cook, tossing the mushrooms in the hot pan, until they are heated through.

Mushrooms

Mushrooms are a metaphor for what I love about food: The best ones are wild and earthy, and they represent infinite possibility. I love mushrooms so much that I felt they deserved their own category on Craft's menu. On a recent jaunt through the Union Square Greenmarket with my son, Dante, I came across some of the most beautiful porcini I had seen since my early years working in France. The mushrooms stopped me dead in my tracks. The man in the stall told me he'd found them growing wild in the Catskill Mountains. We bought his entire stock and hauled them over to Craft. Our guests share my enthusiasm; when hen of the woods mushrooms are available, we can easily go through almost twenty pounds in a day. (Have you ever weighed mushrooms? That's a lot of mushrooms.)

Mushrooms vary so widely, it's hard to give exact rules on choosing them, but whatever variety you choose, look for mushrooms that feel moist and spongy, not dry, when you touch them. Also, try to buy whole mushrooms, and not pieces, which are more likely to have started drying out. Check the bottoms of the mushrooms for pinholes that could indicate worms and weigh them in your hands; they should feel dense. Leave behind the ones that feel light for their size. I recommend wiping the mushrooms with a damp cloth, or scraping the stems clean with a small paring knife, since I think washing mushrooms makes them lose flavor. If you've chosen particularly gritty specimens,

however, dunk the mushrooms into a bowl of standing water, use your hands to gently loosen the dirt, and then lift them out, blotting dry on a clean cloth or paper towel.

One of the great things about mushrooms is that they tell you how best to cook them: Small, firm ones—like cremini, or small chanterelles—will work best in a marinade that would cause larger, softer varieties, like black trumpets or big chanterelles, to fall apart. The larger, meaty varieties—porcini, portobello, hen of the woods—beg to be roasted; their size and heft allow a long enough cooking time for flavors to develop in the pan. Morels are a perfect choice for braising because the mushroom's honeycomb surface acts like a sponge for the flavorful mushroom-butter sauce that forms while they cook. If pressed, I guess I would have to choose porcinis as my overall favorite mushroom. Their great, nutty flavor and meaty texture make them especially versatile; they stand up to all of the techniques mentioned above.

Braised morels

MORELS, WITH THEIR *distinctive appearance and nutty earth flavor, appear wild in the spring. We like to braise the morels slowly at Craft in a bit of beurre fondue. The butter sauce becomes infused with the liquid that the mushrooms give off, yielding a decadent and effortless sauce. I especially recommend serving morels with the other ingredients that appear for a short span in the early spring, such as ramps and peas.*

Serves 6

1 POUND FRESH MOREL
MUSHROOMS

¾ CUP (*1½ sticks*) UNSALTED
BUTTER, DICED

KOSHER SALT AND FRESHLY
GROUND BLACK PEPPER

1 SPRIG FRESH THYME

Clean the morels by trimming off the ends of the stems and wiping them gently with a towel. (If the mushrooms are particularly gritty, give them a quick rinse, then gently towel-dry.) Cut any particularly large mushrooms in half.

Bring about ½ inch of water to a simmer in a medium saucepan over medium heat. Reduce the heat to medium-low. Whisk the butter into the simmering water a piece at a time. Season the resulting beurre fondue with salt and pepper, then add the mushrooms a handful at a time. Stir to coat the mushrooms with the beurre fondue. Add enough water so the braising liquid comes about halfway up the mushrooms. Add the thyme and gently simmer the morels, stirring occasionally, until they are soft and tender, about 20 minutes. Adjust the seasoning with salt and pepper.

Black truffle

FOR OBVIOUS REASONS *this is not an everyday dish, but for a special occasion it can be a dazzler, lending a truly special touch to roasted meat or fish, or dressing up a classic Bordelaise sauce. The black truffles we buy at Craft come from Périgord, in France, with a season that runs from December through February. There is no hard and fast rule about the number of truffles to buy per person. One medium-sized truffle, about 1½ inches in diameter, served in its braising liquid, should make a delicious and aromatic garnish, used sparingly, for four.*

Ingredients	Method

1 BLACK TRUFFLE about 2 cups CHICKEN STOCK KOSHER SALT AND FRESHLY GROUND BLACK PEPPER MAKES 1	Clean the truffle by first rubbing it with a damp towel, then brushing it with a wet toothbrush. Place the truffle in a small pot. Cover with chicken stock, season with salt and pepper, and bring to a simmer over medium heat. Gently simmer the truffle until it softens, about 25 minutes. Drain the truffle, reserving the cooking liquid. Crush the truffle with the back of a spoon. Add just enough of the reserved liquid to soften the crushed truffle. Heat gently and serve.

Marinated lobster mushrooms

LOBSTER MUSHROOMS *are named for their bright orange-red color, which resembles a lobster's shell. Lobster mushrooms are especially good for the dual preparation of this recipe; their dense and meaty texture holds up nicely first to braising and then to the marinating that follows.*

Serves 6

For the mushrooms

6 TABLESPOONS EXTRA-VIRGIN OLIVE OIL

3 POUNDS LOBSTER MUSHROOMS, TRIMMED AND THICKLY SLICED

KOSHER SALT AND FRESHLY GROUND BLACK PEPPER

2 SHALLOTS, PEELED AND MINCED

2 LARGE GARLIC CLOVES, PEELED AND MINCED

3 TABLESPOONS FRESH THYME LEAVES

For the marinade

½ CUP EXTRA-VIRGIN OLIVE OIL

2 LARGE LEEKS, WHITE PARTS ONLY, HALVED LENGTHWISE AND THINLY SLICED

1 YELLOW ONION, PEELED, QUARTERED, AND THINLY SLICED

2 SMALL CARROTS, PEELED AND THINLY SLICED

3 CELERY STALKS, PEELED AND THINLY SLICED

KOSHER SALT AND FRESHLY GROUND BLACK PEPPER

1 GARLIC CLOVE, PEELED

1 BAY LEAF

1 TABLESPOON CORIANDER SEEDS

3 TABLESPOONS SHERRY VINEGAR

⅓ CUP BROWN CHICKEN STOCK (*page 251*)

3 SPRIGS FRESH THYME

3 SPRIGS FRESH FLAT-LEAF PARSLEY

For the mushrooms: Heat a large skillet over medium heat. Add about 1 tablespoon of the oil, then a large handful of the mushrooms (just enough to loosely cover the bottom of the pan). Salt and pepper the mushrooms and let them sizzle undisturbed until the undersides begin to brown, about 2 minutes. Turn each mushroom slice over, then add a little of the minced shallot and garlic and the thyme (use an amount of each of these ingredients proportionate to the percentage of the mushrooms in the pan). Continue cooking the mushrooms until they are tender, moving them around in the pan from time to time, about 2 minutes more. Transfer the mushrooms to a plate lined with a paper towel to drain. Wipe out the skillet and repeat until all the mushrooms have been cooked.

For the marinade: Wipe out the skillet and heat over medium-low. Add 3 tablespoons of the oil, then the leeks, onion, carrots, and celery. Salt and pepper the vegetables, then sweat them, turning them once or twice, until they begin to soften, about 10 minutes. Add the garlic, bay leaf, and coriander seeds and cook until the vegetables are fully tender, about 15 minutes more.

Add the mushrooms, season liberally with black pepper, then add the vinegar. Allow the vinegar to come to a simmer, then add the stock, thyme, and parsley. Simmer the mushrooms, turning them in the liquid, for 2 minutes, then remove the pan from the heat. Add the remaining olive oil and set aside to cool. Once cool, cover and refrigerate for at least 2 hours before serving. Serve at room temperature.

Porcini in parchment

COOKING VEGETABLES *in parchment allows all of the juices to stay within the dish, which makes for great flavor. In this recipe we give the mushrooms color by searing them first in a hot pan before wrapping them in the parchment to finish cooking.*

Serves 6

12 LARGE PORCINI MUSHROOMS

2 TABLESPOONS PEANUT OIL

2 SPRIGS FRESH ROSEMARY

2 SPRIGS FRESH THYME

KOSHER SALT AND FRESHLY
GROUND BLACK PEPPER

3 CLOVES OF GARLIC CONFIT
(*page 259*)

1 TABLESPOON EXTRA-VIRGIN
OLIVE OIL

1 TABLESPOON AGED BALSAMIC
VINEGAR

Heat the oven to 400°F. Trim the ends of the mushroom stems. Peel the stems and wipe the caps with a clean, damp cloth. Leave the mushrooms whole or cut into pieces.

Heat the oil in a large skillet over high heat. Add the mushrooms, rosemary, and thyme and season with salt and pepper. Cook, stirring frequently, until the mushrooms begin to color, 3 to 5 minutes.

Fold six pieces of parchment in half and cut each into a large oval, leaving the folded side straight and uncut (aluminum foil will also work). Place 2 mushrooms in the center of each piece of parchment. Divide the garlic confit, olive oil, and balsamic vinegar evenly among the mushroom packets, then fold and seal. Place the parchment packages on a baking sheet and bake until the mushrooms are tender and fragrant, about 5 minutes.

Porcini risotto

ALTHOUGH I CAN GET dogmatic at Craft about using fresh ingredients, in this recipe we use dried porcini. After reconstituting, you're left with a wonderful mushroom-flavored stock, which is then used in cooking the risotto; this adds just one more layer of flavor to the finished dish.

Serves 6

9 CUPS CHICKEN STOCK

1 CUP DRIED PORCINI MUSHROOMS

1 TABLESPOON EXTRA-VIRGIN OLIVE OIL

4 TABLESPOONS UNSALTED BUTTER

1 YELLOW ONION, DICED

3 CUPS ARBORIO RICE

1 CUP DRY WHITE WINE

KOSHER SALT AND FRESHLY GROUND BLACK PEPPER

FRESHLY GRATED PARMIGIANO-REGGIANO CHEESE TO TASTE

Bring 1 cup of the chicken stock to a simmer in a saucepan over medium-high heat. Add the mushrooms. Remove from the heat and set the mushrooms aside until they soften. Drain the mushrooms, reserving the stock. Strain the reserved stock through a fine strainer, then finely chop the mushrooms. Add the chopped mushrooms to the mushroom-flavored stock.

Bring the remaining 8 cups of chicken stock to a simmer in a saucepan. Allow the stock to reduce by about 1 cup, then keep warm over low heat.

Combine the oil and 1 tablespoon of the butter in a large, high-sided skillet. Heat over medium heat until the butter foams. Add the onion and cook until it is translucent, about 15 minutes. Stir in the rice,

thoroughly coating it with the onion, butter, and oil. Cook the rice until it is no longer chalky looking and begins to pop, about 5 minutes. Add the wine and simmer, stirring constantly until it has evaporated.

Add 1 cup of the warm chicken stock. Simmer, stirring, until the rice is almost dry. Repeat twice more. Stir the mushroom-flavored stock into the rice. Cook, stirring, until the rice is dry again.

Finish cooking the rice by stirring in enough additional warm chicken stock, a cup at a time, so the rice is just barely tender. Stir in the remaining 3 tablespoons of butter. Adjust the seasoning with salt and pepper and add cheese to taste.

Family Meal

May 8
4:00 P.M.

A LINE OF SERVERS, chic in minimalist dark shirts and matching slacks, help themselves to plates of risotto, greens, rabbit stew. They sit at a grouping of rear tables and reach for wineglasses that await them, each holding an ounce or so of "mystery wine" poured from an unmarked decanter. The staff is about to begin a nightly ritual led by Matthew McCartney, Craft's wine director, in which they are challenged to identify the unnamed wine, using visual cues as well as aroma and taste. This develops an intuitive understanding of wine for the servers, and helps them to guide the guests through their own wine choices. As they eat, the

staff swirls and sniffs tonight's mystery white, commenting with that mixture of cynicism and good humor unique to waiters. Matthew takes the floor, inviting observations. A captain opens with a description of color: "Pale to medium straw yellow. Pretty clear and uncloudy . . ." Other servers chime in.

"Slightly watery rim. So not too young."

"I get petrol on the nose. And pears."

"And loads of minerals. Definitely not chardonnay."

The group tastes in unison, and a server comments, "It has balanced acid, but it tastes . . . not sweet,

exactly, but . . . off-dry. Gewürztraminer?"

Matt seems pleased at the guess, but Katie, the general manager, pipes up, "It doesn't have enough lichee to be Gewürz—"

"But it's definitely Germanic," someone says, further narrowing the field. The group unanimously agrees upon something other than chardonnay or sauvignon blanc, the usual suspects of French and American wines. This continues until the wine is finally revealed to be a 1989 Auslese Serrig Herrenberg by Bert Simon. Fully half of the staff admits to thinking this all along. More than one actually did.

The wine discussion segues into other concerns of the day. Katie stands and reminds everyone that restaurant week is fast approaching, when lunch is offered at a promotional price of $20.02. It's a brutal week from the waiter's standpoint, requiring a strong back and an even better disposition. The waiters listen, jot notes, go back for seconds of risotto. Marco appears and talks the staff through menu changes: Ramps and peas are in full swing at the green market, so are morels. He brings a plate of hen of the woods mushrooms for the staff to taste, which they do, passing the heap-ing plate along to the next person, Craft style. Tom pops in and listens. He spears a last mushroom as the dish is carried off to the kitchen. "I like the staff to taste the food and talk about it at family meal. Then they can speak knowledgeably with the guest." Once a month, the staff is encouraged to eat at Craft, on the house, the tradeoff being the detailed survey they fill out immediately after, describing the din-ing experience in true insider fashion. "We get great feedback that way," says Tom. "The waiters will be the first to point out that music levels need adjusting, that the restrooms need picking up late at night. They make great suggestions." Finally Victor, the service director, reminds the busboys to always offer the guest tap water first, and bottled water only as a sec-ond choice. "This tells them that ordering tap water is okay with us." The busboys nod. Got it.

Suddenly Katie checks her watch. 5:00 P.M. In a flash the servers stand, tucking in shirts, whisking away plates, and setting the tables for the evening to come. Another family meal is over, and another larger one—this time with guests—is about to begin.

potatoes

Boulangère potatoes 164

Potato purée 167

Potato gratin 168

Roasted fingerling
   potatoes 170

Fingerling potato salad 171

Gnocchi 172

Stewed potatoes 176

Sweet potato purée 177

5.

Boulangère potatoes

TRADITIONALLY IN FRANCE, *boulangère potatoes were cooked slowly in the baker's oven (the boulangerie) after the day's bread was baked. The potatoes were placed under a rack lined with the villagers' evening roasts, poised to collect the tasty drippings from above. This is a top-of-stove interpretation that captures the meaty flavor of the original.*

Serves 6

2½ POUNDS SMALL FINGERLING POTATOES (*about 30*), PEELED

ABOUT 1 QUART VEAL STOCK (*page 252*)

1 BUNCH FRESH THYME PLUS 2 TABLESPOONS PICKED LEAVES

KOSHER SALT AND FRESHLY GROUND BLACK PEPPER

½ POUND SMOKED BACON

2 YELLOW ONIONS, PEELED

Place the potatoes in a large pot. Add enough veal stock to cover. Add the bunch of thyme and season with salt and pepper. Bring the stock to a simmer over medium heat and cook until the potatoes begin to soften, about 15 minutes. Cool the potatoes in the stock uncovered.

Cut the bacon into thin 1-inch strips (lardons). Cut the onions into pieces about the same size as the bacon. Render the bacon in a very large skillet over medium-low heat. When the bacon begins to crisp, about 15 minutes, add the onions and season with salt and pepper. Raise the heat to medium and cook, stirring occasionally, until the onions are golden, about 25 minutes.

Using a slotted spoon, lift the potatoes out of the stock and into the skillet (if the pan is too crowded, divide the onion mixture and potatoes between 2 pans). Reserve the stock. Add the thyme leaves and a generous amount of pepper and heat over medium heat. Add ¼ cup of the reserved veal stock. Turn the potatoes in the simmering stock, glazing them as the stock reduces. Repeat several times until the potatoes are evenly coated and fully tender (expect to use 1 to 2 cups of veal stock in all). Adjust the seasoning with salt and pepper and serve.

Potato purée

ONE OF MY FAVORITE *cooking stories is that of the great French chef Joël Robuchon who, despite a lifetime of preparing intricate and dazzling meals, won his reputation for his amazing potato purée. A major goal of mine when opening Craft was to create the best potato purée anyone had ever tasted—silky, light, and full of flavor. Soon after the restaurant opened, a food writer called to tell me the dish had sparked a debate among chefs in San Francisco: What did I put in Craft's version to make it so sweet? The answer: nothing. Use only Yukon gold potatoes. Despite being a pain in the neck to work with, these are the sweetest potatoes of all.*

Serves 6

10 LARGE YUKON GOLD POTATOES (*about 5 pounds*), SCRUBBED

KOSHER SALT AND FRESHLY GROUND WHITE PEPPER

1 CUP MILK

1 CUP HEAVY CREAM

½ CUP (*1 stick*) UNSALTED BUTTER, SOFTENED

3 TO 4 TABLESPOONS EXTRA-VIRGIN OLIVE OIL (*optional*)

2 TABLESPOONS CHOPPED FRESH CHIVES (*optional*)

Place the unpeeled potatoes in a large pot. Add water to cover. Season generously with salt and pepper and bring to a simmer over medium heat. Simmer until the potatoes are tender; begin checking them after 20 minutes. Drain the potatoes, then while they are still hot, peel them (hold the potato with a dish towel and use a sharp paring knife). Place the peeled potatoes in a covered bowl or pot so they remain hot.

Purée the potatoes by pressing them through a fine-holed ricer. Return the purée to the pot. Whisk the purée with a stiff whisk. Gradually whisk in the milk, cream, and butter, then season with salt and white pepper. Serve dressed with extra-virgin olive oil and chopped chives, if desired.

Potato gratin

THE WORD gratin *comes from the French word for a baking dish, and refers to anything layered into a dish and cooked, either under a broiler or in an oven, usually until the top browns. The key to this recipe is choosing a baking dish that can hold the potatoes in dense, even layers (too large a pan will make it hard to gauge how much cream to add). Be sure to layer the potatoes snugly and systematically; if they are haphazardly arranged, they will not cook evenly.*

Serves 6

8 MEDIUM RUSSET POTATOES
(*about 6 pounds*)

1½ QUARTS HEAVY CREAM

6 SPRIGS FRESH THYME

4 CLOVES GARLIC CONFIT
(*page 259*), CHOPPED

KOSHER SALT AND FRESHLY
GROUND WHITE PEPPER

Peel the potatoes. Slice them about ⅛ inch thick (this is most easily done with a mandoline). Put the potatoes into a large pot and add the cream, thyme, garlic, salt, and pepper. Slowly bring the potatoes to a simmer over medium-low heat (this will take 1 to 1½ hours). Remove the pot from the heat.

Heat the oven to 350°F. Pour a thin layer of the cream used to cook the potatoes into the bottom of a medium baking or gratin dish (an 8-inch round will work). Using a slotted spoon, gently lift the potatoes into the baking dish, breaking as few potatoes as possible. Snuggly fit the potatoes into the dish in layers and press them down with the back of a spoon. Pour in only enough cream so that when you press down on the potatoes cream coats the exposed top layer (about 2 cups). Bake the gratin until the top is browned and bubbly, about 40 minutes, then serve.

Roasted fingerling potatoes

FINGERLING POTATOES are named for their shape and size—roughly that of a human thumb. They are particularly suited to roasting because they hold their shape well and the skin—more delicate than that of a standard russet potato—crisps nicely during cooking. Roasted fingerlings make a perfect accompaniment to roasted chicken or meat and are delicious with a dipping sauce of garlicky aïoli.

Serves 6

4 TABLESPOONS OLIVE OIL

3 POUNDS FINGERLING POTATOES, SCRUBBED AND HALVED LENGTHWISE

KOSHER SALT AND FRESHLY GROUND BLACK PEPPER

4 SPRIGS FRESH ROSEMARY

1 CUP AÏOLI (*page 256*) (*optional*)

Heat the oven to 375°F. Heat 2 large ovenproof skillets over medium-high heat. Divide the oil between the pans, then add the potatoes, cut side down. Salt and pepper the potatoes and let the pans regain heat. Transfer the pans to the oven, then cook the potatoes until the first sides are golden, about 6 minutes. Turn the potatoes and add 2 sprigs of rosemary to each pan. Continue cooking the potatoes until they are fully tender, about 8 minutes longer. Serve immediately, with aïoli, if desired.

Fingerling potato salad

WHAT IS MOST *distinctive about this salad is that the potatoes—small fingerlings—are left whole. Cooking them gently allows the potatoes to acquire a beautiful creamy texture.*

Serves 6

5 SHALLOTS, PEELED

4 POUNDS SMALL FINGERLING POTATOES, SCRUBBED BUT NOT PEELED

12 BLACK PEPPERCORNS

4 SPRIGS FRESH THYME

KOSHER SALT

1 LARGE CELERY STALK

¼ POUND SLAB BACON

¼ CUP AÏOLI (*page 256*)

2 TABLESPOONS CHAMPAGNE VINEGAR

2 TABLESPOONS DIJON MUSTARD

2 TABLESPOONS CHOPPED MIXED FRESH HERBS SUCH AS FLAT-LEAF PARSLEY, TARRAGON, AND CHERVIL

Finely dice 3 of the shallots, cutting them into ⅛-inch dice (brunoise); reserve. Slice the remaining shallots and place them in a large pot. Add the potatoes, peppercorns, thyme, and a generous amount of salt. Fill the pot with enough water to cover the potatoes and bring to a boil over low heat. When the water boils cover the pot and remove it from the heat. Allow the potatoes to cool in the covered pot, about 25 minutes. Drain and peel.

Dice the celery and the bacon. Put the celery and shallots in a large mixing bowl. Render the bacon in a medium skillet over medium heat. Drain the crisped bacon. Add the bacon and the potatoes to the mixing bowl and mix gently.

In a separate bowl mix the aïoli with the vinegar and mustard. Season with salt and pepper. Dress the potatoes with the aïoli mixture. Mix the herbs into the salad and serve.

Gnocchi

WILLIAM GRIMES *of the* New York Times *called these gnocchi "light-weight, butter-laden eye-rolling pleasure bombs." The secret to light, flavorful gnocchi is that the potatoes need to be as dry as possible, which means baking them for a long time, then cutting them right away to release steam. The potatoes also shouldn't be seasoned until the last moment, since salt can trap moisture. Use a fine-holed potato ricer and be sure to cut and fold the ingredients to mix, rather than kneading. Overhandling the dough can make the gnocchi tough.*

Serves 6 to 8

9 RUSSET POTATOES (*about* 6½ *pounds*), SCRUBBED

FRESHLY GROUND WHITE PEPPER

1 EGG YOLK

ABOUT 2¾ CUPS FLOUR PLUS ADDITIONAL FOR DUSTING

KOSHER SALT

¾ CUP (1½ *sticks*) BUTTER, DICED

FRESHLY GRATED PARMIGIANO-REGGIANO

Heat the oven to 350°F. Prick the potatoes with a fork. Bake the potatoes until they are soft, about 1½ hours.

Cut the hot potatoes in half. Scoop the potato out of the skin and into a fine-holed ricer. Pass the potatoes through the ricer onto a clean work surface then using a pastry scraper chop them as they cool. When the potatoes are cool season them generously with white pepper.

Beat the egg yolk and drizzle it over the potatoes. Measure 1¼ cups of the flour and sprinkle this over the potatoes. Cut the flour and egg yolk into the potatoes until

they resemble coarse crumbs. Bring the mixture together into a ball.

Sprinkle a scant ¼ cup of flour on the work surface. Spread the potato mixture over the flour, then top with another scant ¼ cup. Using the scraper then your hands, fold and press the dough until the flour is incorporated. Repeat. If the dough still feels tacky, repeat once more, this time covering the table and the dough each with 2 tablespoons of flour.

Roll the dough into a compact log. Dust the outside with flour, then allow the dough to rest for about 5 minutes. Lightly dust the work surface with flour. Divide the dough into 8 pieces. Roll each section into a log about ½ inch thick. Using a floured knife or pastry cutter, cut the dough into gnocchi about 1 inch long.

Bring a pot of heavily salted water to a boil. Working in two or three batches, drop the gnocchi into the water and cook, stirring occasionally, until they float, 2 to 3 minutes. Drain the gnocchi then refresh them in ice water. Drain them, place them on a baking sheet, cover with plastic wrap, and refrigerate until ready to serve. Gnocchi should not be made more than 6 hours before they are to be served.

Bring ½ inch of water to a simmer in a medium saucepan over medium heat. Reduce the heat to medium-low and whisk in the butter a piece at a time. Add the gnocchi to the beurre fondue and stir gently to coat them with sauce as they warm. Season with salt and white pepper and serve topped with grated cheese.

Stewed potatoes

THE LONG, SLOW COOKING *of the potatoes in this dish allows them to absorb plenty of flavor from the tomatoes and herbs. I recommend Yukon gold potatoes, although any of the high-starch, non-waxy varieties will work. Yukon golds tend to be drier, so they'll release plenty of starch into the dish and take on the most flavor during cooking.*

Serves 6

4 LARGE YUKON GOLD POTATOES
(*about 2 pounds*), PEELED

2 TABLESPOONS OLIVE OIL

4 WHOLE PEELED PLUM TOMATOES
(*canned or fresh*)

1 LARGE GARLIC CLOVE, PEELED

KOSHER SALT

1 TABLESPOON FINELY CHOPPED
FRESH ROSEMARY

1 TABLESPOON FINELY CHOPPED
FRESH SAGE

CRACKED BLACK PEPPER

½ CUP CHICKEN STOCK

Dice the potatoes, cutting them about 1 inch square. Place the olive oil in a large pot and heat over medium-low. Add the potatoes, then crush the tomatoes and add them with their juices. Mince the garlic as fine as possible with a little salt. Add the garlic–salt paste to the pot. Add the rosemary and sage, season with salt and pepper, and mix well.

Pour in the chicken stock, partially cover the pot, and cook, stirring occasionally, over low heat, until the potatoes are tender, about 40 minutes. Adjust the seasoning with salt and pepper and serve.

Sweet potato purée

THE SWEET POTATOES *in this recipe are roasted first, which intensifies their flavor, before being whisked with butter.*

Serves 6

4 LARGE SWEET POTATOES

1 CUP (*2 sticks*) UNSALTED BUTTER

PINCH OF FRESHLY GRATED NUTMEG

KOSHER SALT AND FRESHLY GROUND BLACK PEPPER

Heat the oven to 325°F. Place the sweet potatoes on a baking sheet and cook until soft, about 1½ hours. Split the sweet potatoes in half. Scoop all the potatoes into a fine-holed food mill set over a large saucepan. Discard the skins. Purée the potatoes, then whisk over low heat, gradually adding the butter. Season the potatoes with nutmeg, salt, and pepper and serve.

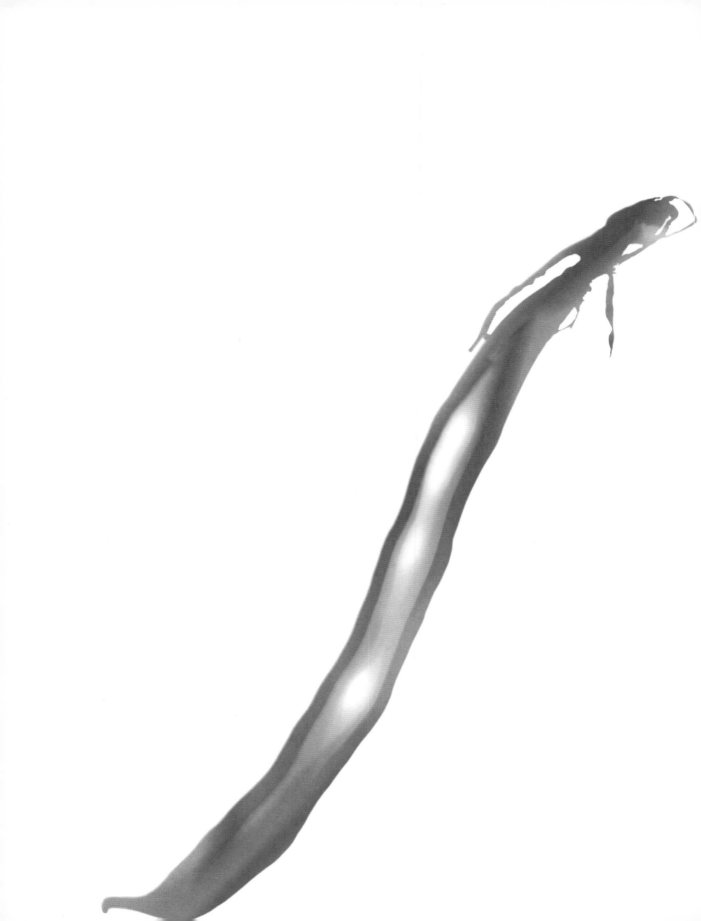

grains + beans

Farro	180
Polenta	181
Fava beans	183
Braised romano beans	184
Cannellini beans	185
Cranberry beans	186

Farro

FARRO IS AN "HEIRLOOM" Italian wheat, in other words an original strain that hasn't been crossbred over time. I like its earthy flavor and the distinct texture of the grains. Farro makes an especially nice accompaniment to succulent cuts of meat like Braised Rabbit (page 65), soaking up the rich juices so that none are lost. If you find yourself with leftovers, add some good olive oil and fresh herbs and toss the farro with tomatoes and cucumber for a delicious salad the next day.

Serves 6

¼ POUND PANCETTA, IN ONE PIECE

1 TABLESPOON EXTRA-VIRGIN OLIVE OIL

1 YELLOW ONION, PEELED AND QUARTERED

1 CELERY STALK, CUT IN HALF

2 MEDIUM CARROTS, PEELED AND HALVED

KOSHER SALT AND FRESHLY GROUND BLACK PEPPER

2 CUPS FARRO

4 SPRIGS FRESH ROSEMARY AND 4 SPRIGS FRESH THYME TIED TOGETHER IN CHEESECLOTH

ABOUT 6 CUPS CHICKEN STOCK

2 CUPS PAN-ROASTED DICED VEGETABLES *(page 263)* *(optional)*

Dice the pancetta. Add the olive oil to a large pot and heat over medium. Add the pancetta and render it, about 10 minutes. Add the onion, celery, carrots, salt, and pepper. Increase the heat to medium-high and cook, stirring occasionally, until the vegetables are tender and golden, about 10 minutes. Rinse the farro and add it to the pot. Stir to coat with oil, then add the herb bundle and enough chicken stock to cover by about 1 inch. Bring the stock to a simmer, then reduce the heat to low, partially cover, and cook, stirring occa-sionally, until the farro is tender, about 20 minutes.

Drain the farro, reserving the cooking liquid. Spread the farro out on a baking sheet to cool. Pick out the vegetables and herb bundle, then refrigerate the farro until shortly before serving. Warm the farro with a little of the reserved stock (start with ¼ cup and add more stock or water if the pan is too dry). Add the diced roasted vegetables (if using) and adjust the sea-soning with salt and pepper.

Polenta

AT CRAFT *we buy polenta from Anson Mills, in South Carolina, which sells a fresh-milled organic corn with a coarser grind than traditional polenta. We like the heartier texture this imparts to the dish; it stands up well to braised meats and rich sauces. Anson Mills is available in many gourmet markets, where it's refrigerated to stave off fermentation. To find a retailer who carries it near you, try www.ansonmills.com, or see Resources, page 269, for their phone and fax numbers.*

Serves 6

6 CUPS CHICKEN STOCK

2 CUPS POLENTA

KOSHER SALT AND FRESHLY GROUND BLACK PEPPER

8 TABLESPOONS (*1 stick*) UNSALTED BUTTER

Bring the stock to a boil over high heat in a large saucepan. Whisking constantly, gradually add the polenta in a thin stream. Whisk until the polenta comes to a simmer, then reduce the heat to medium low. Season with salt and pepper and gently simmer, stirring frequently with a wooden spoon, until the polenta no longer tastes grainy, about 45 minutes. Stir in the butter, adjust the seasoning with salt and pepper, and serve.

Fava beans

THE FAVA BEANS *in this recipe are cooked with a small amount of tarragon "tea." This allows us to introduce the flavor of tarragon into the dish, without dark specks of the herb marring the bright green fava purée.*

Serves 6

4 SPRIGS FRESH TARRAGON, PLUS
1 TABLESPOON FRESH CHOPPED
LEAVES FOR GARNISH

7 CUPS SHELLED FAVA BEANS (*about
10 pounds in the pod*)

KOSHER SALT

FRESHLY GROUND BLACK PEPPER

2 TABLESPOONS UNSALTED
BUTTER, DICED

3 TABLESPOONS EXTRA-VIRGIN
OLIVE OIL

Combine the tarragon sprigs and 1 cup of water in a small saucepan. Bring to a boil over high heat. Cover the pot, remove it from the heat, and allow it to steep for about 15 minutes, then strain.

Blanch the fava beans in boiling salted water until the peels are loosened and the beans tender, about 3 minutes. Refresh the beans in ice water, then peel them.

Place ½ cup of the fava beans in a blender or food processor. Add ½ cup of the tarragon tea and purée. Continue adding tea until the purée is the consistency of a creamy vinaigrette, about ¼ cup more. Season the purée with salt and pepper.

Combine the beans and purée in a saucepan and warm over medium-low heat. Whisk in the butter a little at a time. Adjust the seasoning if necessary. Serve topped with the chopped tarragon and extra-virgin olive oil.

Braised romano beans

Romano beans are thick, meaty, and satisfying. This long, gentle braise is an opportunity to infuse the beans with the rich, underlying flavors of soffritto.

Serves 6

1 CUP BLONDE SOFFRITTO BASE
(page 255)

1 GARLIC CLOVE, PEELED AND
CRUSHED

2 SPRIGS FRESH ROSEMARY

1 TEASPOON TOMATO PASTE

4 WHOLE PEELED PLUM TOMATOES
(canned or fresh)

KOSHER SALT AND FRESHLY
GROUND BLACK PEPPER

1½ POUNDS ROMANO BEANS, ENDS
TRIMMED THEN HALVED

Heat the soffritto in a large high-sided skillet over medium heat. Add the garlic and rosemary and cook until fragrant, about 5 minutes. Add the tomato paste, then crush the tomatoes and add them with their juices. Season the mixture with salt and pepper and simmer, stirring occasionally, until the tomatoes and juice mix with the soffritto, about 5 minutes. Add the beans and ½ cup water. Bring the liquid to a simmer. Stir to coat the beans, salt them, then cover the pan and reduce the heat to low. Gently braise the beans, stirring once or twice, until they are fully tender, about 45 minutes. Adjust the seasoning with salt and pepper and serve.

Cannellini beans

THE TRICK TO MAKING *these beans wonderful is to cook them very, very slowly. Start them off with cold water, and keep the heat as low as it will go under the pot. The exact cooking time depends on a variety of factors, including the size and the age of the beans, so start checking them for tenderness after 45 minutes. Let the beans cool in their cooking liquid so that they continue to absorb the flavorful cooking liquid (otherwise they'll dry out as they release steam).*

Serves 6

2 CUPS DRIED CANNELLINI BEANS, SOAKED OVERNIGHT

3 TABLESPOONS EXTRA-VIRGIN OLIVE OIL PLUS ADDITIONAL FOR GARNISH

2 GARLIC CLOVES, PEELED AND CRUSHED

2 SPRIGS FRESH SAGE

KOSHER SALT

Drain the beans. Place the oil, garlic, and sage in a large pot (a rondeau—a large round pot with straight sides about 5 inches high—is best, but a soup pot will work). Warm the oil over low heat. When the garlic is fragrant, about 5 minutes, add the beans. Stir to coat with oil, then add enough cold water to cover by about 2 inches. Add salt and increase the temperature to medium low. Cook the beans very gently (occasional small bubbles) until they are tender throughout, about 1½ hours. Allow the beans to cool in the cooking liquid. Reheat or serve at room temperature dressed with extra-virgin olive oil.

Cranberry beans

As with many of the dishes at Craft, the cranberry beans here are served in a "sauce" made of themselves (in this case, puréed cranberry beans) as a way of further emphasizing the taste of the beans and holding them together in an elegant, flavorful way.

Serves 6

¼ POUND PANCETTA, IN ONE PIECE

1 TABLESPOON EXTRA-VIRGIN OLIVE OIL

1 YELLOW ONION, PEELED AND QUARTERED

1 CELERY STALK, CUT IN HALF

2 MEDIUM CARROTS, PEELED AND HALVED

KOSHER SALT AND FRESHLY GROUND BLACK PEPPER

6 CUPS SHELLED FRESH CRANBERRY BEANS (*about 2½ pounds in the pod*)

4 SPRIGS OF FRESH ROSEMARY AND 4 SPRIGS OF FRESH THYME TIED TOGETHER IN CHEESECLOTH

ABOUT 1½ QUARTS CHICKEN STOCK

Dice the pancetta. Add the olive oil to a large pot and heat over medium. Add the pancetta and render it, about 10 minutes. Add the onion, celery, carrots, salt, and pepper. Increase the heat to medium-high and cook, stirring occasionally, until the vegetables are tender and golden, about 10 minutes.

Add the beans to the pot. Stir to coat with oil, then add the herb bundle and enough chicken stock to cover by about ½ inch. Bring the stock to a simmer, then reduce the heat to medium-low and cook gently until the beans are tender, about 35 minutes. Remove the beans from the heat and allow them to cool in the cooking liquid.

Drain the beans, reserving the cooking liquid. Spread the beans out on a baking sheet to cool. Pick out the vegetables and herb bundle. Transfer ½ cup of the beans to a food processor. Purée, adding enough reserved cooking liquid to smooth to the consistency of a creamy vinaigrette, about ¾ cup.

To serve, combine the purée and beans in a saucepan and warm over low heat. Add a little additional cooking liquid if the beans are too dry (start with ¼ cup) and adjust the seasoning with salt and pepper.

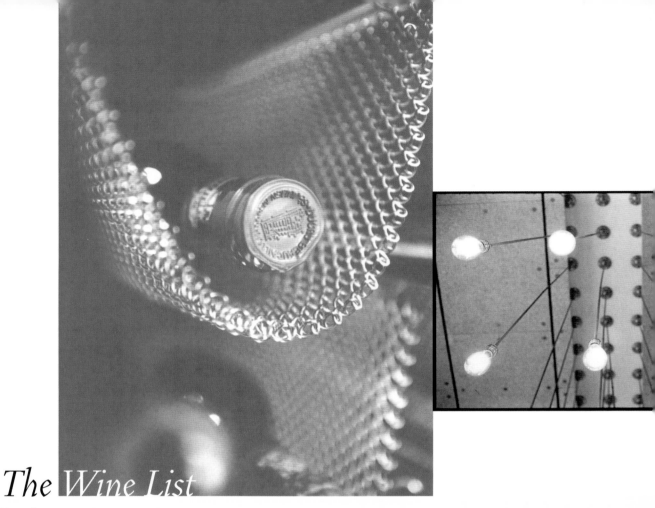

The *Wine List*

November 12, 2002
5:15 P.M.

MATTHEW MCCARTNEY leaves family meal and climbs the steps to Craft's iron catwalk, clipboard in hand, to take a swift wine inventory before service. Matthew is Craft's wine and beverage director. He is responsible for wine purchasing, cellar management, staff education, and all the other beverages at Craft, including beer, Cognac, ports, liquors, spirits, coffee, and a tea list to rival that of Claridge's, in London. At night he walks the floor at Craft, interacting with guests, opening wine, and playing the traditional role of sommelier. "Diners today are much more sophisticated than they once were," he explains. "They used to ask for a glass of white or red. Now they ask by varietal—they say, 'What kind of chardonnay do you have?' or 'Can

you bring me a glass of syrah?'"

Building the wine list at Craft began with conceptual questions, Matthew recalls, before the restaurant's opening. "'Single ingredient' presentation and artisan foods were a driving concept behind the menu—did that mean we should buy nothing but wines made from one grape, no blends? Buy only American wine? Or stick to artisans who make only a few barrels a year? Tom and I had a lot of discussion back and forth about this." Ultimately they decided against these ideas since the resulting restrictions would have made fair pricing of an extensive wine-by-the-glass program impossible. "Also," Matthew explains, "I started to ask myself, Is a Lafitte-Rothschild any less artisanal because they make

twenty-five thousand cases?" If buying wine that way meant ignoring some of the best wine available, then it defeated Craft's purpose and became no more than a gimmick.

Instead, Matthew and Tom decided to keep Craft's wine focus on high-quality, unique wines wherever they may come from. "I think my willingness to taste everything on equal footing is what ends up making our list great. I don't feel a need to fill the list with 'name' wines, only great wine, and the result is that we end up serving great quality at fair prices."

A big part of Matthew's job is training the staff. "We hold nightly wine tastings at family meal as well as monthly wine chats where we sit down as a group to taste and discuss wine.

Doing that encourages a wine dialogue among the servers and helps them feel confident discussing what guests really want to know: What does the wine taste like?" He focuses obsessively on keeping wine service as relaxed and unpretentious as possible. No cork-and-swirl theatrics. No spewing arcane information. No "pushing" pricey bottles. In the staff manual he writes, in big letters, IT'S ONLY WINE!

Matthew comes to wine from an atypical place—the kitchen. He started out as a cook, working at Daniel, as well as at kitchens in France and Italy. It was during a *stage* in Tuscany—home of chianti and Brunello di Montalcino—that Matthew discovered a passion for wine. Fast-forward to an eighteen-month vinicultural tour of Italy, begin-

ning in Emilia-Romagna, moving into Florence (where, coincidentally, he crossed paths with Marco Canora, Craft's future chef), and ending up in Chianti, working the 1996 harvest at Castello di Verrazzano. Matthew tried every job at the winery, including working the crusher, pitching yeast, and "pumping over," a process in which wine from the bottom of the cask is brought up and over the "cap" of grape skins in order to extract color. He even volunteered to climb into the 100-hectoliter tanks to shovel out pips and skins left from fermentation—a tough, stinky job that is said to cause at least one or two deaths each year from carbon dioxide poisoning.

Back in his Daniel days, Matthew had met Tom and discussed his goal to

move from the kitchen to the "front of the house," specifically into managing a wine program of his own. When Matthew returned to the United States, Tom hired him to assist Paul Grieco, then wine director at Gramercy Tavern as a precursor to working at Craft. From Paul he learned the basics of cellar management; how to rotate wines, and how to keep abreast of the wine world through tastings and auctions, while managing a complicated and lively wine and beverage program. When Tom opened Craft, Matthew lobbied for the job of wine director. "Tom could see my passion for wine, and my culinary background meant a lot to him; he understands the synergy between great wine and great food. Each one makes the other taste better."

dessert

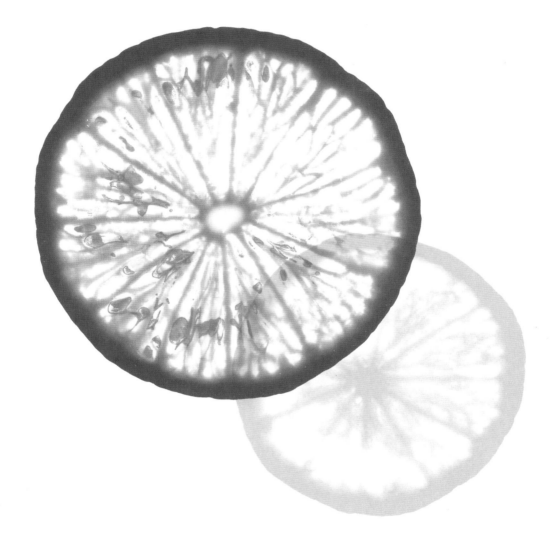

Ice cream/sorbet

Vanilla ice cream	223
Hazelnut ice cream	225
Caramel ice cream	226
Maple ice cream	227
Banana sorbet	230
Pineapple sorbet	231
Concord grape sorbet	232
Blood orange sorbet	234
Sour cherry sorbet	235

Compotes

Blueberry compote	236
Raspberry compote	237
Apricot compote	238
Sour cherry compote	239

Confections

Caramel popcorn	240
Peanut brittle	242
Strawberry jellies	243

Sauces and Sides

Chilled Sauternes sabayon	244
Chocolate sauce	245
Caramel sauce	246
Passion fruit sauce	247

Pastry

Apricot tarte tatin	192
Almond pound cake	193
Banana upside-down cake	195
Warm chocolate tart	196
Cinnamon cake doughnuts	199
Apple fritters	200
Brioche	201
Pain perdu	202
Almond biscotti	204
Chocolate biscotti	205
Pine nut biscotti	206
Pistachio biscotti	208

Custard

Coconut panna cotta	209
Lemon steamed pudding	211
Steamed toffee pudding	212

Roasted

Pan-roasted apples	218
Pan-roasted peaches	219
Roasted bananas	220

Poached

Poached pears	221
Poached rhubarb	222

Apricot tarte tatin

TARTE TATIN *is a classic French tart named after the signature dessert at the Hôtel Tatin in the Loire Valley. The classic dish, credited to the Tatin sisters, who operated the hotel, uses apples, but tarte Tatin lends itself well to substitution. We recommend you experiment with whatever fruit— peaches, nectarines, pineapples—are fresh and readily available. We've included a Craft kitchen recipe for puff pastry (page 267), but making it is an unwieldy process. This is one of the rare recipes in which a store-bought ingredient can be easily substituted without noticeable compromise to the final dish.*

Makes one 10-inch tart

14 OUNCES PUFF PASTRY, PAGE 267 (*defrosted commercial puff pastry will also work*)

¾ CUP SUGAR

1½ TABLESPOONS UNSALTED BUTTER, DICED

10 TO 12 APRICOTS, HALVED AND PITTED

Heat the oven to 350°F. Roll out the puff pastry on a floured work surface into an 11-inch circle.

Combine the sugar and about 2 table-spoons water (enough so the mixture looks like damp sand) in a 10-inch cast-iron skillet. Heat over high heat, swirling the pan occasionally, until the sugar caramelizes. When the caramel is amber, whisk in the butter one piece at a time. Remove the pan from the heat and fit the apricots cut side up in a single layer. Lay the pastry over the apricots and gently tuck the sides of the dough into the pan.

Bake the tart until the crust is puffed and golden, about 40 minutes. Cool for at least 1 hour in the pan. Just before serving, heat the tart for 10 minutes in a 350°F. oven. Unmold and serve warm.

Almond pound cake

THIS RECIPE MAKES *a rich but simple cake that is delicious served with ice cream, fruit compotes, or roasted fruit. If almond flour is unavailable, coarsely grind ²/₃ cup of whole, peeled almonds in a food processor, then add the all-purpose flour called for in the recipe and process until finely ground.*

Makes 1 loaf cake

1 CUP (*2 sticks*) UNSALTED BUTTER, SOFTENED

¾ CUP SUGAR

1 TEASPOON VANILLA EXTRACT

3 LARGE EGGS

²/₃ CUP ALMOND FLOUR (*see head note*)

1 CUP CAKE FLOUR

1 TEASPOON BAKING POWDER

½ TEASPOON KOSHER SALT

Heat the oven to 325°F. Cream the butter with the sugar and vanilla in a mixer. Add the eggs one at a time. Sift the almond flour with the cake flour, baking powder, and salt. Add the flour mixture to the butter and mix until combined.

Spoon the batter into a buttered 9¾ × 3 × 3-inch loaf pan and bake until the cake is golden and a toothpick inserted in the center is clean when withdrawn, about 30 minutes. Remove the pan from the oven and allow it to cool for 10 minutes. Turn it out of the pan onto a rack and cool completely before cutting and serving.

Banana upside-down cake

THIS RECIPE IS KIN *to the Apricot Tarte Tatin. Like that recipe, this one can be varied throughout the year by substituting seasonal fruits when they are at their prime. Try it paired with Banana Sorbet (page 230).*

Makes one 8-inch cake

3 SMALL TO MEDIUM BANANAS

2 CUPS SUGAR

4 TABLESPOONS (*1/2 stick*) UNSALTED BUTTER

1½ CUPS ALL-PURPOSE FLOUR

2 TEASPOONS BAKING POWDER

½ TEASPOON KOSHER SALT

⅓ CUP CLARIFIED BUTTER (*see note*)

2 EGGS

½ CUP BUTTERMILK

2 TEASPOONS VANILLA EXTRACT

Heat the oven to 325°F. Cut the bananas in half lengthwise, then cut each piece in half crosswise. In a saucepan, combine 1 cup of the sugar with about 2 tablespoons water (enough so the mixture looks like damp sand). Melt over high heat, swirling the pan occasionally, until the sugar caramelizes. When the caramel is a dark amber add the butter. Pour the caramel into an 8-inch cake pan and allow to set for 3 to 5 minutes. Arrange the bananas in the caramel, cut side down, in a single layer.

Sift the flour with the baking powder and salt and set aside. In a mixer, using the whisk attachment, combine the remaining cup of sugar and the clarified butter. With the mixer on low, add the eggs one at a time. Add the buttermilk and vanilla. Add

the flour mixture to the batter a third at a time. Pour the batter over the bananas and bake until the cake springs back and begins to pull away from the sides, about 50 minutes. Allow the cake to cool for 5 minutes, then unmold it onto a serving plate. Serve warm or at room temperature.

Note

To make clarified butter, bring ½ cup butter to a simmer in a saucepan over medium heat. Remove the pan from the heat and skim off the butter solids that have risen to the top. Set the butter aside in a warm place for about 30 minutes, and then carefully decant the butter into a measuring cup, stopping short of pouring any of the solids at the bottom of the pan.

Warm chocolate tart

THIS TART IS TRICKY *but delicious. Be careful not to overbeat the butter for the dough or the tart shell will sag and crack. Also save enough dough scraps for use as patches should the need arise.*

Makes one 9½-inch tart

For the crust

2¼ CUPS ALL-PURPOSE FLOUR, PLUS ADDITIONAL FOR DUSTING

½ CUP COCOA POWDER

PINCH OF KOSHER SALT

1¼ CUPS (2½ *sticks*) UNSALTED BUTTER, SOFTENED

½ CUP PLUS 2 TABLESPOONS SUGAR

1 EGG

For the filling

5 OUNCES EXTRA-BITTER CHOCOLATE, CHOPPED

3 TABLESPOONS UNSALTED BUTTER, CUT INTO SMALL PIECES

3 TABLESPOONS HEAVY CREAM

2 EGGS, AT ROOM TEMPERATURE

1 EGG YOLK, AT ROOM TEMPERATURE

5 TEASPOONS SUGAR

For the crust: Sift the flour with the cocoa and salt. Combine the butter with the sugar in a mixer and mix on low speed. Add the egg and mix just until incorporated. Mix the dry ingredients into the butter mixture by hand. Form the dough into a ball, flatten it, then wrap in plastic and chill for at least 1 hour.

Working quickly, on a large piece of lightly floured parchment paper roll out the dough into a thin circle about 13 inches across. Place the parchment paper on a baking sheet, cover the dough with plastic, and chill it for at least 1 hour.

Carefully fit the dough into a 9½-inch tart shell with a removable bottom. Shape the dough to fit the bottom and sides without stretching or pinching it. Freeze the dough for at least 1 hour.

Heat the oven to 350°F. Bake the crust until it puffs, about 10 minutes, level it by pressing with a measuring cup, then continue baking until the crust is crisp, about 10 minutes more. Set aside to cool. Keep the oven at 350°F.

For the filling: Combine the chocolate, butter, and cream in a metal or glass bowl set over simmering water. Whisk until the chocolate and butter melt. Remove the pot from the heat but continue to keep the mixture warm by resting it over the hot water.

Meanwhile, whisk the eggs with the egg yolk in a mixer set at low speed until foamy, then add the sugar. Increase the speed to medium-high and continue whisking until the mixture is pale and doubled in volume, about 3 minutes.

Working quickly, fold half the egg mixture into the warm chocolate. Fold the remaining chocolate into the batter. Pour the filling into the crust and bake until the filling has risen and begins to crack, 15 to 20 minutes. Serve immediately.

Cinnamon cake doughnuts

The doughnuts at Craft have been immensely popular since pastry chef Karen DeMasco put them on the menu.

Makes about 24

For the cinnamon sugar

½ CUP SUPERFINE SUGAR

¾ TEASPOON GROUND CINNAMON

PINCH OF GROUND CARDAMOM

PINCH OF KOSHER SALT

For the doughnuts

3½ CUPS CAKE FLOUR

1 CUP SUGAR

1 TEASPOON BAKING SODA

2 TEASPOONS BAKING POWDER

¾ TEASPOON KOSHER SALT

1½ TEASPOONS GROUND CINNAMON

½ TEASPOON FRESHLY GRATED NUTMEG

¾ CUP BUTTERMILK

⅓ CUP CLARIFIED BUTTER (*page 195*)

1 EGG

3 EGG YOLKS

PEANUT OIL FOR DEEP-FRYING

For the cinnamon sugar: Combine the superfine sugar, cinnamon, cardamom, and salt in a bowl and mix well.

For the doughnuts: Fit a mixer with the paddle attachment. Sift 1½ cups of the cake flour with the sugar, baking soda, baking powder, salt, cinnamon, and nutmeg into the mixer bowl. With the mixer running, gradually add the buttermilk, butter, egg, and egg yolks. When the mixture is smooth fold in the remaining 2 cups of flour by hand.

Divide the dough in half. Roll the first half out about ⅛ inch thick on a well-floured surface. Using a 2-inch cutter, cut out about 12 rounds. Then, using a ¾-inch cutter, cut out the centers. Repeat with the remaining dough.

Place about 4 inches of oil in a deep saucepan and heat to 375°F. Fry the doughnuts and holes in batches without crowding. Turn the doughnuts so they brown on all sides. Cook until they are evenly browned, 2 to 4 minutes per batch. Drain on paper towels. Roll the warm doughnuts in the cinnamon sugar and serve.

Apple fritters

MOST BATTERS *for fritters call for the addition of a carbonated beverage, such as club soda, for leavening. In this recipe we get the same effect by using beer, which also adds a nice, hoppy flavor to the fritters. The recipe specifies lager, which tends to have a lighter flavor than an ale.*

Makes 20 to 30

⅔ CUP LAGER

2 LARGE EGGS, SEPARATED

1½ TEASPOONS CLARIFIED BUTTER (*page 195*), MELTED AND COOLED

3 TABLESPOONS SUGAR

½ TEASPOON VANILLA EXTRACT

1 CUP ALL-PURPOSE FLOUR

½ TEASPOON KOSHER SALT

½ TEASPOON GROUND CINNAMON

4 FIRM TART APPLES, SUCH AS GRANNY SMITH

PEANUT OIL FOR DEEP-FRYING

1 CUP SUGAR MIXED WITH 1 TEASPOON GROUND CINNAMON (*optional cinnamon sugar*)

Whisk the lager with the egg yolks, butter, sugar, and vanilla. Sift the flour with the salt and ½ teaspoon cinnamon, then whisk the mixture into the batter. Set the batter aside to rest for 30 minutes.

Beat the egg whites until they hold soft peaks, then fold them into the batter. Peel and core the apples. Heat 2 to 3 inches of oil to 375°F. in a large saucepan.

Slice the apples about ¼ inch thick. Working in batches, coat the apples with batter and fry them without crowding until the fritters are puffed and golden, about 1½ minutes per side. Serve warm plain or dusted with cinnamon sugar.

Brioche

ON ITS OWN, *brioche is a classic breakfast bread, light but rich-tasting, that is delicious with nothing more than a cup of good, strong coffee. At Craft we use it as the basis for pain perdu, an eggy French-toast-like cake that is one of the most popular items on the dessert menu. Karen DeMasco, Craft's pastry chef, bakes her brioche in cans to give it the neat, round slices she prefers for pain perdu (see photograph, page 203). To do this, fill a clean, empty coffee can (label removed) with dough to just under one quarter full, cover with plastic wrap, and allow to rise, as below. Remove the plastic wrap and bake until the top is lightly browned and the brioche is springy.*

Makes one 9 x 5-inch loaf

2 TEASPOONS ACTIVE DRY YEAST

2 TABLESPOONS SUGAR

2⅓ CUPS BREAD FLOUR

2 LARGE EGGS

1 LARGE EGG YOLK

1½ TEASPOONS KOSHER SALT

1 CUP (*2 sticks*) COLD, UNSALTED BUTTER, DICED

Combine the yeast, 1½ teaspoons of the sugar, and 2 tablespoons warm (not hot) water in a small bowl. Set aside for 10 minutes.

Mix the flour with the remaining 4½ teaspoons sugar in an electric mixer fixed with the paddle attachment. At low speed, mix in the whole eggs. Increase the speed slightly and add the yeast mixture, then the egg yolk and salt. Gradually add the butter. When the butter has been incorporated, form the dough into a ball and place it in a large oiled bowl. Cover with plastic wrap and set aside to rise in a warm place for about 2 hours (the dough will rise but not double). Punch the dough down, return it to the bowl, cover with plastic, and refrigerate overnight.

Heat the oven to 350°F. Place the dough in a 9 × 5-inch loaf pan. Cover the dough with plastic wrap and allow it to warm to room temperature and rise until it fills the pan. Bake the brioche, uncovered, until the crust is lightly browned and the loaf springy, about 40 minutes. Cool for 10 minutes, then remove from the pan and cool completely.

Pain perdu

One of the most popular desserts at Craft is pain perdu, an eggy, rich cake—essentially French toast—made from brioche soaked in sweet custard. It works equally well served with ice cream or roasted fruit, or all by itself.

Serves 4 to 8

1 CUP HEAVY CREAM

1 CUP MILK

6 TABLESPOONS SUGAR

2 EGGS

2 EGG YOLKS

¾ TEASPOON VANILLA EXTRACT

1 LOAF OF BRIOCHE *(page 201)*

3 TABLESPOONS CLARIFIED BUTTER *(page 195)*

CONFECTIONERS' SUGAR *(optional)*

Combine the cream, milk, and 3 tablespoons of the sugar in a saucepan and warm over medium heat, while whisking. When the sugar melts remove the pan from the heat. Beat the eggs with the egg yolks and the remaining 3 tablespoons of sugar, then temper them by whisking in about ½ cup of the warm cream mixture. Whisk the tempered eggs back into the cream mixture. Strain the custard through a fine sieve, stir in the vanilla extract, then chill.

Heat the oven to 250°F. Slice the brioche about 1¼ inches thick. Coat 2 or 3 slices with the custard. Meanwhile heat the butter in a large skillet over medium heat. Cook the brioche in the butter until the brioche is golden and warmed through, about 3 minutes per side. Transfer the cooked slices to the oven to keep warm. Repeat until all the brioche has been cooked. Serve warm, dusted with confectioners' sugar, if desired, with roasted fruit or ice cream.

Almond biscotti

At Craft we serve many different types of biscotti. I've included recipes for four of them in this book, each with a different flavor and texture. These almond biscotti are crisp and nutty, and a particular favorite of mine. They should last about 2 to 3 weeks in airtight containers. They also freeze well and can be refreshed easily by placing in a 200° F. oven for 20 minutes.

Makes about 60 cookies

¾ CUP CHOPPED ALMONDS

½ CUP (*1 stick*) UNSALTED BUTTER, SOFTENED

1 CUP SUGAR

2 LARGE EGGS

1½ TABLESPOONS ANISEED

1½ CUPS ALL-PURPOSE FLOUR

½ TEASPOON BAKING POWDER

½ CUP YELLOW CORNMEAL

¼ TEASPOON KOSHER SALT

¾ CUP GOLDEN RAISINS

Heat the oven to 325°F. Spread the almonds on a baking sheet and toast until golden and fragrant, about 10 minutes.

In a mixer fitted with the paddle attachment, cream the butter with the sugar. Add the eggs, one at a time, then add the aniseed. Sift the flour with the baking powder, cornmeal, and salt. With the mixer running on low, gradually add the dry ingredients. Fold the raisins and the almonds into the dough.

Cover 2 baking sheets with parchment. Form the dough into four 8-inch logs, place 2 on each sheet pan, and bake until firm, about 40 minutes. Cool for at least 10 minutes, then slice each log into about 15 biscotti.

Reduce the oven temperature to 200°F. Arrange the biscotti on a baking sheet and toast them until they are dry and golden, about 2 hours. Cool and serve.

Chocolate biscotti

HAZELNUTS, BROWN SUGAR, *and espresso give these chocolate biscotti rich character. Like most biscotti, these will keep nicely in an airtight container for 2 to 3 weeks, and will freeze well if you find yourself with extras.*

Makes about 30

1⅓ CUPS HAZELNUTS, CHOPPED

1½ CUPS ALL-PURPOSE FLOUR

6 TABLESPOONS COCOA POWDER

½ CUP PLUS 1 TABLESPOON DARK BROWN SUGAR

5 TABLESPOONS GRANULATED SUGAR

¼ TEASPOON BAKING SODA

¼ TEASPOON KOSHER SALT

4 TEASPOONS UNSALTED BUTTER, SOFTENED

3 LARGE EGGS

1 TEASPOON VANILLA EXTRACT

1 TABLESPOON STRONGLY BREWED ESPRESSO

Heat the oven to 325°F. Spread the hazelnuts out on a baking sheet and toast until golden and fragrant, about 15 minutes.

Combine the flour, cocoa, brown sugar, granulated sugar, baking soda, and salt in a mixer fitted with the paddle attachment. With the mixer on low, add the butter, then the eggs, vanilla, and espresso. Fold in the hazelnuts, then form the dough into 2 logs. Place the logs on a parchment-lined baking sheet and bake until they are firm, 30 to 40 minutes. Cool, then slice each log into about 15 biscotti.

Reduce the oven temperature to 200°F. Place the biscotti on a baking sheet and toast until dry, about 2 hours. Cool and serve.

Pine nut biscotti

THESE ARE NOT *conventional biscotti. They are very "short" (buttery) and not overly sweet. This makes them a great complement to sweeter items like ice cream or caramelized fruit. If almond flour is unavailable, coarsely grind ²/₃ cup of whole, peeled almonds in a food processor, then add the all-purpose flour called for in the recipe and process until finely ground.*

Makes about 30

1½ CUPS PINE NUTS

¾ CUP (*1¹/₂ sticks*) UNSALTED BUTTER, SOFTENED

3 TABLESPOONS SUGAR

2 LARGE EGGS

MINCED ZEST OF 1 ORANGE

1 TEASPOON VANILLA EXTRACT

½ CUP ALMOND FLOUR (*see head note*)

1¼ CUPS ALL-PURPOSE FLOUR

1½ TEASPOONS BAKING POWDER

Heat the oven to 325°F. Place the pine nuts on a baking sheet and toast until golden, 10 to 15 minutes.

In a mixer fitted with the paddle attachment, cream the butter with the sugar. Add the eggs, orange zest, and vanilla. Sift the almond flour with the all-purpose flour and the baking powder. With the mixer running on low, gradually add the flours. Fold in the nuts.

Line a baking sheet with parchment paper. Divide the dough into 2 equal parts. Form the dough into 8-inch logs. Bake until firm, 30 to 40 minutes. Cool for at least 10 minutes, then slice each log into 15 biscotti.

Reduce the oven to 200°F. Arrange the biscotti on baking sheets and toast until golden, 1½ to 2 hours.

Pistachio biscotti

SINCE BISCOTTI KEEP *so well, we recommend making a variety with different textures and flavors, like chocolate (see page 205) and pine nut (see page 206) and these delicious pistachio biscotti, ahead of time. Serve them together as an assortment, like we do at Craft.*

Makes about 30

¾ CUP SHELLED, UNSALTED PISTACHIOS

¾ CUP SUGAR

1¼ CUPS ALL-PURPOSE FLOUR

½ CUP CORNMEAL

¾ TEASPOON BAKING SODA

¼ TEASPOON KOSHER SALT

2 LARGE EGGS

3½ TABLESPOONS UNSALTED BUTTER, MELTED

MINCED ZEST OF 1 ORANGE

Heat the oven to 325°F. Spread the pistachios on a baking sheet and toast until fragrant, about 10 minutes.

In a mixer fitted with the paddle attachment, combine the sugar, flour, cornmeal, baking soda, and salt. With the mixer on low, add the eggs, then the melted butter. Fold in the orange zest and pistachios.

Raise the oven temperature to 350°F. Form the dough into 2 logs and place on a parchment-lined baking sheet. Bake until firm and golden, about 20 minutes. Cool slightly, then slice each log into about 15 cookies.

Reduce the oven to 200°F. Arrange the biscotti on the baking sheet and toast until dry, about 1½ hours. Cool and serve.

Coconut panna cotta

Panna cotta is Italian for "cooked cream." Ours is a lighter, refreshing take on the classic dish that substitutes coconut milk for cream. At Craft, my pastry chefs crack coconuts to extract the milk. Here we use unsweetened canned coconut milk instead. I recommend serving this dessert with tart Passion Fruit Sauce (page 247).

Serves 8

1 ¼-OUNCE PACKET OF POWDERED
GELATIN

2 CUPS MILK

¾ CUP SUGAR

¼ TEASPOON KOSHER SALT

13.5 OUNCES UNSWEETENED
COCONUT MILK (*1 can*)

Sprinkle the gelatin over ¼ cup of the milk and set aside for 10 minutes. Combine the remaining 1¾ cups milk, the sugar, and the salt in a saucepan and bring to a simmer over medium heat, stirring occasionally. Remove the pan from the heat. Whisk first the gelatin mixture then the coconut milk into the pan. Strain the panna cotta mixture through a fine sieve then pour it into eight 4-ounce ramekins or coffee cups; chill overnight. The panna cotta can be served as is or unmolded (run a warm knife around the edge of each, then turn onto chilled plates).

Lemon steamed pudding

THESE LIGHT, DELICIOUS *puddings can be made ahead and then reheated in a water bath before unmolding and serving. They've been popular since Craft opened, and they work particularly well with a side of fresh blueberries or with Blueberry Compote (page 236).*

Serves 6

½ CUP SUGAR PLUS ADDITIONAL FOR DUSTING RAMEKINS

2 EGGS, SEPARATED

3 TABLESPOONS PLUS 1 TEASPOON ALL-PURPOSE FLOUR

PINCH OF KOSHER SALT

⅔ CUP BUTTERMILK

2½ TABLESPOONS FRESH LEMON JUICE

FINELY CHOPPED ZEST OF 1½ LEMONS

Heat the oven to 300°F. Butter and lightly sugar six 4-ounce ramekins. Beat the egg whites until they hold soft peaks, then set them aside. Sift the sugar with the flour and salt. In a mixer, using the whisk attachment, combine the buttermilk, lemon juice, egg yolks, and lemon zest. Gradually add the flour mixture, then fold in the egg whites. Divide the batter among the prepared ramekins. Place the puddings in a water bath (set the ramekins in a larger pan; fill the pan with enough hot water to come halfway up the ramekins) and cover with aluminum foil. Bake until the puddings rise and are almost firm, about 25 minutes, then uncover and continue baking until the tops are lightly golden and the puddings spring back when touched, about 15 minutes more. Unmold and serve warm alone, with fresh berries, or with berry compote.

Steamed toffee pudding

At Craft we make small steamed puddings in individual ramekins. For home presentation, we think a larger, shared pudding works better. The extra effort of this dessert is worth it; our guests take a bite and react the way they do to foie gras (moan out loud with pleasure). This and the Lemon Steamed Pudding on page 211 are two of the biggest sellers at Craft.

Makes one 8-inch pudding

For the pudding

8 OUNCES PITTED DATES
(ABOUT 9 LARGE MEDJOOL)

1 TEASPOON VANILLA EXTRACT

1 TEASPOON BAKING SODA

4 TABLESPOONS (*½ stick*)
UNSALTED BUTTER, SOFTENED

1 CUP SUGAR

1 LARGE EGG

¾ CUP PLUS 2 TABLESPOONS
ALL-PURPOSE FLOUR

1 TEASPOON BAKING POWDER

½ TEASPOON KOSHER SALT

For the sauce

2 TABLESPOONS UNSALTED BUTTER

½ CUP HEAVY CREAM

6 OUNCES DARK BROWN SUGAR

¼ TEASPOON KOSHER SALT

1½ TEASPOONS DARK RUM

For the pudding: Heat the oven to 325°F. Blanch the dates in boiling water long enough to loosen their skins. Cool the dates in ice water, then peel them. Chop them in a food processor. With the machine running, gradually add 1 cup water and purée.

Transfer the date paste to a saucepan and bring to a simmer over medium heat. Add the vanilla, then remove the pan from the heat and whisk in the baking soda.

In a mixer fitted with the paddle attachment, cream the butter with the sugar, then beat in the egg. Sift the flour, baking powder, and salt together, then add one third of this mixture to the sugar and butter. Mix in one third of the date paste. Repeat, alternating between the flour mixture and date paste, until both are incorporated.

Butter an 8-inch cake pan. Fit a piece of parchment into the bottom. Pour the batter into the pan and set the pan in a larger pan. Fill the outer pan with enough very hot water to come about three fourths of the way up the sides of the cake pan. Cover with aluminum foil and bake until the outer edges of the pudding are firm and brown and the middle is still somewhat wet, 45 minutes to 1 hour.

For the sauce: Combine the butter, cream, brown sugar, salt, and rum in a saucepan. Bring to a simmer over medium-high heat, stirring frequently.

Remove the foil from the pudding. Using a skewer, poke holes all over the top of the pudding (30 to 40 in all). Slowly drizzle about ¾ cup of the warm sauce over the top of the pudding, allowing the pudding to absorb the sauce as you pour. Keep the rest of the sauce warm in a pan set over very low heat. Recover the pudding and bake until it is firm throughout (like a cake) and the sauce has caramelized on the top, about 30 minutes. Remove the cake from the oven and allow it to cool for 10 minutes. Turn it over onto a plate. Serve warm in wedges accompanied by additional sauce.

Dinner Service

November 14
5:45 P.M.

CRAFT IS SHORT A FISH COOK tonight, so executive chef Marco Canora has stepped in to prep tuna, fresh off the boat. He slices cleanly into the bright red fillet; it offers the resistance of, say, Jell-O. "We'll serve this raw, with just olive oil and sea salt, maybe a little lemon confit on the side," Marco explains to a visiting chef, who is observing for the night. All around him, the kitchen is so clean it's hard to believe that lunch ever happened. "At four-thirty we scrub the place top to bottom. Tom likes dinner to start with a brand new kitchen." Cooks move busily, setting up their stations, finishing last-minute prep. There is a perceptible quickening in the air: Dinner is imminent.

Over in pastry, a cook quickly lifts hot tuiles, whisper-thin lace cookies, from a sheet pan onto a rolling pin where they'll cool. Another roasts pears

in a saucepan of honey, glazing them to a deep amber. The pastry cooks are more relaxed than the rest of the kitchen—for now. "We won't get our first order until around six-thirty, seven o'clock," Anya explains. "So we have time to start our soufflé bases and sorbets for tomorrow. Then at around ten, eleven o'clock, we'll get slammed. Just as those guys"—she nods in the direction of the line—"are finishing up." She hoists a bowl of brioche dough onto her hip and heads for the walk-in, where it will proof overnight.

Victor Salazar, Craft's service director, appears beside Marco, adjusting his tie. He confirms menu changes with the chef before climbing back up the stairs to help the waiters ready their stations. Maryanne, an experienced captain with a gentle manner, has just learned that tonight she'll be waiting on a certain celebrity columnist, a

known curmudgeon. "I picked Maryanne on purpose," says Victor, as he scans the room. "No matter how grumpy a guest is when he walks in the door, by the end of the night she's turned him right around."

7:00 P.M. The kitchen is percolating. Tom appears in his chef coat, having walked over from Gramercy Tavern. He pulls a ticket from the printer. "Give me a monk, a dorade, a risotto, a nut." That's shorthand for butternut squash purée, a cold-weather favorite. "Lamb, medium. Pick it up!" P.J., the meat cook, tips a roasting pan, ladling juices over a loin of lamb, and fires back, "Lamb, picking up!" At P.J.'s elbow is a container of soffritto and another of short-rib braise, a mixture of veal base, *remouillage* (the second, double-strength rendering of veal stock), and red wine, known in the kitchen as *remi*. P.J. turns to a duck breast resting on

his cutting board. He cuts neat, pink slices, each one capped with crisp skin over a layer of pearly fat, and sets aside the duck bones. "We'll use those for duck jus tomorrow," he explains.

With Tom calling out orders, Marco is freed to work on other things; he grabs a pot of monkfish braise begun by the lunchtime saucier and passes it through a food mill, separating out fish bones and vegetables from the flavorful sauce. P. J. walks his plate of sliced lamb to the pass, setting it under the warming lights. Tom presses a finger against the meat and hands it back. "Can you make it hotter?" he asks quietly. Food temperature is a constant issue at Craft; even when plated piping hot, food loses some heat in transit up the stairs to the dining room, and then cools more in the center of the table as guests continue to chat. When they finally do dig in, the food is spooned onto cool plates, losing even more heat in the process. Tom, Marco, and Katie are exploring a way of putting warmed plates in front of guests to help offset the problem, but that's still down the road. Word filters down to the kitchen that Paul Anka has just arrived for dinner. The cooks launch into a spontaneous chorus of Anka tunes, with Dan, nighttime fish cook, scoring points for most obscure lyrics.

8:30 P.M. Upstairs the dining room is humming. Guests settle into their leather chairs, eyeing the wine list, the folks at the next table, the food that goes by. Copper pots are set into the center of tables and lids are lifted, releasing clouds of fragrant steam. A well-known fashion designer occupies her usual table, sketchpad in hand. "She says the restaurant gives her ideas," explains Joao, her waiter, beaming. The room is a blend of familiar faces and a few furrowed brows, new guests who are guided through the unconventional menu by the staff. Monday and Tuesday nights at Craft seem to feature regulars. Fridays and Saturdays are often first-timers and out-of-town guests. Wednesdays and Thursdays, like tonight, are anyone's guess.

Maryanne passes breathlessly. "How is he?" Victor asks, referring to the testy columnist. "He's fine," she laughs, "keeping me running!" Victor smoothly steps into her station as backup, to keep Maryanne's other tables from feeling snubbed. Dolores, the Maître d'hôtel, touches his sleeve as he passes. "I've got a three-top from the *New York Times* that called earlier and upped the reservation to four people. They just walked in, but now they're five." "Can we do it?" Victor asked, scanning the packed room. "I'll do my best," she answers. "But it's going to be tight."

Dinner Service, *continued*

EVEN WHEN PARTIES don't add last-minute guests, the nine-o'clock turn is tricky, Victor explains. Six-thirty reservations—often folks who had asked for a seven-thirty or eight-o'clock table—tend to complete late and linger, setting off a chain of events that inevitably holds up the nine-o'clock tables at the door. Victor hails John, another manager, and nods toward a group seated in the corner. "Keep an eye on table sixty-six," he warns. "They waited twenty minutes for their first course." John peers at the guests in question. "Have they complained?" "No," says Victor. "They're happy, but let's stay on top of it." John nods. He comes to Craft fresh off a sommelier job in Palm Beach, where he also hosted a popular wine show called "Liquid Assets" for the local NPR station. "I'll pop down to the kitchen and check on their entrées."

8:45 P.M. Tom picks up a lobster tail, frowning. The daytime prep cook, whose job it was to parboil the lobster, has overcooked the entire batch. Tom glances up at a ticket and then makes for the floor to find Victor. "Tell the lady on table seventy-four that I can't serve her the braised lobster she ordered," he says. "Ask her to pick anything else on the menu, on us." Victor nods and goes to talk to the guest. Tom pulls John aside. "Eighty-six Lobster," he says, using house shorthand for "We're no longer serving lobster, please spread the word." John spins on his heel and tells two servers, who send the news among their ranks faster than a rumor through a small town.

9:15 P.M. Marco hunches over a log of porchetta, slicing it into perfect rounds alongside veal terrine and dense wedges of rabbit ballottine. Craft's extensive charcuterie is all handmade and house-cured, a point of

pride for Marco. He handles the meats like favored children, spooning truffle vinaigrette over the veal. Tom steps away to visit with guests on the floor. As tickets continue to riff through the printer, sous-chef Damon steps away from the stove and takes his place at the pass, calling out orders. "Chanty, purée" he calls to Scott, who places chanterelles into a hot pan and ladles potato purée into a copper pot. Mushrooms and potatoes are Scott's only responsibilities tonight but those items alone make him the busiest cook on the line. Maryanne pops into the kitchen: One of her guests (guess who?) is asking for his short ribs. Marco glances up at the ticket, surprised. "He ordered it, like, five minutes ago!" Maryanne explains that this guest is, um, *particularly eager* for his food. Marco throws his hands in the air. Maryanne smiles an apology and heads back to the floor.

10:20 P.M. The printer in pastry spits into overdrive. Anya and Rachel work ceaselessly, their faces matching studies in absorption. One pulls hot soufflés from the oven and upends miniature *tartes Tatin* onto plates, while the other dips and scoops from a drawer, using two spoons to form perfect quenelles of ice cream and sorbet. "Pick up!" Anya calls, already onto the next ticket. A runner steps over and hoists the tray onto his shoulder. In a flash he's gone.

11:00 P.M. The dining room is still humming, but the cadence has shifted from frenetic to smooth. The smell of coffee wafts agreeably through the room. A group of businessmen rise with effort from a table by the window, making the necessary adjustments to buttons, waistlines, and neckties. One of them shares a parting joke with the waiter, while Victor watches, pleased. He is protective of his staff, keen to the special demands that Craft-style service places on them. "Carrying heavy trays all night up those steps is hard. And we need at least three—sometimes four— waiters to clear a table, with all these extra plates and copper pots. Typically, it only takes two." Consequently, there are more workers on the floor each night sharing the tip pool. Victor feels this naturally selects for a different type of server, one with more commitment and different motives. "These waiters are special. They care a lot about service, about great food. They care about making the night memorable for people." Case in point: Maryanne's V.I.P. grasps her hand as he follows his guests to the door, planting a gruff kiss on her cheek. "Great meal, great meal, young lady," he murmurs, reaching for his coat. "We'll be back."

11:30 P.M. The cooks break down their stations, wrapping nine-pans tightly in plastic for the walk-in. They're finished for the night, but pastry is still waiting on final orders. "These desserts look simple, but it's misleading," says Anya. The steamed toffee puddings, a big favorite, are a perfect example: Midway through moist baking they must be broken open half way, to allow a mixture of rum, brown sugar, and cream to be poured in the center. The resulting pudding is sticky and hard to unmold, causing more than a few to break before they ever hit the plate. "This looks like just a homely little cake," says Anya, picking one up. "But then you taste it . . ." The printer begins to churn and Rachel reaches for the slip, reading to her partner. "Tatin and a pain perdu, side of roast pears. Banana tart, caramel sauce . . ." The women start again, bending carefully over plates, giving the desserts their full attention, and putting a sweet end to another meal.

Pan-roasted apples

THE APPLES CAN *be cooked ahead of time and reheated in a 350°F. oven for about 3 minutes before adding them to the reduced apple cider. Pan-roasted apples work well alongside the brioche Pain Perdu (page 202) or garnished with Caramel Ice Cream (page 226).*

Serves 6

2 TABLESPOONS CLARIFIED BUTTER (*page 195*), MELTED

3 GRANNY SMITH APPLES, PEELED, CORED, AND SLICED INTO ½-INCH ROUNDS

1 CINNAMON STICK

½ VANILLA BEAN

¼ CUP SUGAR

3 TABLESPOONS UNSALTED BUTTER

⅔ CUP APPLE CIDER

Work in batches. Heat a large skillet over medium-low heat. Brush the pan with clarified butter and add 1 sliced apple (the apple slices should fill the pan in a single layer). Add the cinnamon stick and vanilla bean. Sprinkle the apples with one third of the sugar and cook until the sugar melts, about 10 minutes. Reduce the heat to low, add one third of the butter, and cook until the apple slices are golden on one side, 5 to 10 minutes. Flip the apples and cook until the second sides begin to color, 3 to 5 minutes more. Remove the apples from the pan and set aside on a plate in a warm place (the back of the stove or a low oven). Repeat, reusing the cinnamon and vanilla, until all the apples are cooked.

To serve, increase the heat to medium and deglaze the skillet with the apple cider. Allow the cider to reduce to a syrup, about 5 minutes. Return the apples to the pan and warm them in the syrup. Serve immediately.

Pan-roasted peaches

DRY WEATHER *during the summer of this writing led to an unusually sweet, succulent peach harvest. But pan-roasting peaches will tease out the sugar from even less-than-great specimens.*

Serves 6

ABOUT 2 TABLESPOONS CLARIFIED
BUTTER (*see page 195*), MELTED

3 PEACHES, QUARTERED

1 CINNAMON STICK

½ VANILLA BEAN

¼ CUP SUGAR

3 TABLESPOONS UNSALTED BUTTER

⅔ CUP APPLE JUICE

Work in batches. Heat a medium skillet over medium-low heat. Brush the pan with clarified butter. Add 1 quartered peach. Add the cinnamon stick and vanilla bean. Sprinkle the peaches with one third of the sugar and cook until the sugar melts, about 10 minutes. Reduce the heat to low, add one third of the butter, and cook until the peaches are golden, 5 to 10 minutes. Flip the peaches and cook until the second side begins to color, 3 to 5 minutes more. Remove the peaches from the pan and set aside on a plate in a warm place (the back of the stove or a low oven). Repeat, reusing the cinnamon and vanilla, until all the peaches are cooked.

To serve, increase the heat to medium and deglaze the skillet with the apple juice. Allow the juice to reduce to a syrup, about 5 minutes, then return the peaches to the pan. Warm them in the syrup. Serve immediately.

Roasted bananas

ROASTED BANANAS *are a delicious garnish to Pain Perdu (page 202),*
or spooned, with their caramel, over ice cream. If you'd like to serve them as
your main dessert, you may want to double the recipe.

Serves 6

¼ CUP SUGAR

3 BANANAS

1 TO 2 TABLESPOONS CLARIFIED
BUTTER *(page 195)*

Place the sugar in a small saucepan and
add about 1 tablespoon water (enough
water so the mixture looks like damp
sand). Heat the sugar over high heat,
swirling the pan occasionally, until it melts
and turns amber. Remove the pan from the
heat and whisk in 2 tablespoons of water.

Heat the oven to 350°F. Peel the bananas,
split them lengthwise, then cut each half
into thirds crosswise. Heat a large nonstick

ovenproof skillet over medium-high heat.
Add the clarified butter, then add the
bananas, cut side down. Transfer the skillet to the oven. Roast the bananas until
they are lightly browned, 7 to 10 minutes.
Flip the bananas, add the caramel, and
continue roasting until the bananas are
golden and the syrup is slightly thickened,
about 7 minutes more. Baste the bananas
with the caramel and serve warm.

Poached pears

POACHED PEARS *are delicious served alongside Caramel Ice Cream (page 226) or Almond Pound Cake (page 193). These are a great make-ahead dish as the pears should be chilled before serving.*

Makes 6

2 CUPS DRY WHITE WINE

2 CUPS SUGAR

1 TEASPOON GRATED ORANGE ZEST

½ VANILLA BEAN

1 BAY LEAF

6 BARTLETT PEARS

Combine the wine, sugar, zest, vanilla, and bay leaf in a large pot. Add 1½ quarts of water and bring to a boil over high heat.

Meanwhile, peel, halve, and core the pears. Lower the heat under the poaching liquid, add the pears, and cover them with a piece of parchment paper (to keep them submerged). Gently simmer until the pears are tender, about 20 minutes (cooking time will vary depending upon the ripeness of the pears). Remove the pot from the heat and allow the pears to cool in the poaching liquid. Serve the pears chilled, moistened with poaching liquid.

Poached rhubarb

THIS TECHNIQUE *will work just as well with kumquats—another fruit that, like rhubarb, needs to be cooked to be appreciated. Simply quarter and seed the kumquats and poach, as below, until the fruit is tender. Poached rhubarb and poached kumquats are both delicious served over homemade Vanilla Ice Cream (page 223).*

Makes about 3 cups

1 POUND RHUBARB (*3 large stalks*)
2½ CUPS SIMPLE SYRUP
(*page 266*)

1 VANILLA BEAN, HALVED

Cut the rhubarb in ½-inch dice. Put the simple syrup in a large saucepan. Scrape the vanilla bean into the simple syrup and bring the mixture to a simmer over medium high. Add the rhubarb and allow the syrup to return to a simmer. Cover the rhubarb directly with parchment paper and remove the pan from the heat. Allow the rhubarb to cool to room temperature. Serve or chill in the poaching liquid.

Vanilla ice cream

FOR BEST RESULTS *with this ice cream I strongly urge vanilla beans over extract. They are pricey, but they have a much greater depth of flavor. Also, the seeds of the vanilla bean will permeate the base, lending their flavor to each bite. For lemon verbena ice cream add 2 or 3 sprigs of fresh lemon verbena to the yolk and cream mixture. Chill overnight before straining.*

Makes about 1¹/₂ quarts

2 CUPS HEAVY CREAM

2 CUPS WHOLE MILK

1 VANILLA BEAN, SPLIT

1¼ CUPS SUGAR

9 EGG YOLKS

Place the cream and milk in a medium saucepan. Scrape the vanilla seeds from the pod into the cream mixture, add the pod and ¾ cup of the sugar, and bring to a rolling boil over medium-high heat, stirring occasionally.

Meanwhile whisk the remaining ½ cup of sugar with the egg yolks until well mixed. Temper the yolks by gradually whisking in about ½ cup of the hot cream mixture. Whisk the tempered yolks into the remaining cream mixture and strain the mixture through a fine sieve into a metal bowl or pot set over ice (this prevents the yolks from overcooking).

Chill the ice cream base thoroughly, then process it in an ice cream maker according to the manufacturer's directions. Transfer the ice cream to a container and let it firm for at least 2 hours in the freezer before serving.

Hazelnut ice cream

THESE SWEET, *rich, acorn-size nuts become very fragrant once they are toasted. In this recipe we steep the ground nuts in the ice cream base overnight to get their flavor, then strain them out before processing. If you like nuts in your ice cream, leave the nuts in the base. If you are a fan of pistachios, substitute unsalted pistachios for the hazelnuts for an equally delicious ice cream.*

Makes about 1½ quarts

1 CUP HAZELNUTS

2 CUPS HEAVY CREAM

2 CUPS WHOLE MILK

1¼ CUPS SUGAR

⅛ TEASPOON VANILLA EXTRACT

9 EGG YOLKS

PINCH OF KOSHER SALT

Heat the oven to 350°F. Place the nuts on a baking sheet and toast until fragrant and golden, about 15 minutes. Finely grind the nuts and reserve.

Place the cream and milk in a medium saucepan. Add ¾ cup of the sugar and the vanilla and bring to a rolling boil over medium-high heat, stirring occasionally.

Meanwhile whisk the remaining ½ cup of sugar with the egg yolks until well mixed.

Temper the yolks by gradually whisking in about ½ cup of the hot cream mixture. Add the tempered yolks to the remaining cream mixture and whisk. Stir in the salt and ground nuts. Set the pan over ice to cool, then chill overnight.

Strain the ice cream base through a fine sieve, then process in an ice cream maker according to the manufacturer's directions. Transfer the ice cream to containers and freeze for at least 2 hours before serving.

Caramel ice cream

THE CARAMEL *for this dish should be as dark as possible—nearly smoking—to impart the most flavor to the ice cream. As our pastry chef, Karen DeMasco, says, "It should stink your house up!" If the ice cream base breaks, purée it with a hand mixer or in a blender before transferring it to the ice cream machine. Caramel ice cream is delicious with Apple Fritters, page 200.*

Makes about 1½ quarts

1½ CUPS SUGAR

2 CUPS HEAVY CREAM

2 CUPS WHOLE MILK

⅛ TEASPOON VANILLA EXTRACT

9 EGG YOLKS

PINCH OF KOSHER SALT

Place 1¼ cups of the sugar in a large saucepan and dampen with about 1 tablespoon of water (enough so the mixture looks like damp sand). Cook over high heat, swirling the pan until the sugar melts and the caramel is very dark (and nearly smoking).

Remove the pan from the heat and carefully whisk in the cream, then the milk. Return the pan to the heat, add the vanilla, and bring to a rolling boil, whisking occasionally.

Meanwhile whisk the remaining ¼ cup of sugar with the egg yolks until well mixed.

Temper the yolks by gradually whisking in about ½ cup of the hot cream mixture. Add the tempered yolks to the remaining cream mixture and whisk. Add the salt, whisk, then pass the ice cream base through a fine strainer into a metal bowl or pot set over ice (this prevents the yolks from overcooking).

Chill the ice cream base thoroughly, then process it in an ice cream maker according to the manufacturer's directions. Transfer the ice cream to containers and let it firm for at least 2 hours in the freezer before serving.

Maple ice cream

MAPLE ICE CREAM *is wonderful paired with roasted fall fruits like apples and pears.*

Makes about 1 quart

2 CUPS HEAVY CREAM

2 CUPS WHOLE MILK

⅛ TEASPOON VANILLA EXTRACT

1¼ CUPS MAPLE SUGAR

PINCH OF KOSHER SALT

9 EGG YOLKS

Place the cream and milk in a medium saucepan. Add the vanilla and ¾ cup of the maple sugar and bring to a simmer over medium-high heat, stirring occasionally.

Meanwhile whisk the remaining ½ cup of maple sugar and the salt with the egg yolks until well mixed. Temper the yolks by gradually whisking in about ½ cup of the hot cream mixture. Add the tempered yolks to the remaining cream mixture and whisk. Strain the ice cream base through a fine strainer into a metal bowl or pot set over ice (this prevents the yolks from overcooking).

Chill the ice cream base thoroughly, then process it in an ice cream maker according to the manufacturer's directions. Transfer the ice cream to containers, then let it firm for at least 2 hours in the freezer before serving.

Sorbets and compotes

Just like everything else on the dinner menu at Craft, dessert items are ordered singly, but here that approach seems to be met with particular glee by our guests—almost as though they've been invited to the adult version of a make-your-own-sundae bar!

The pastries on Craft's dessert menu remain more or less the same throughout the year. The fruits (which like meat or fish are grouped according to preparation), on the other hand, tell the story of the changing seasons and are offered in a variety of forms; poached or roasted, or as sorbets or compotes. The sorbets have been particularly popular since Craft opened; sour cherry (page 235), banana (page 230), pineapple (page 231), and blood orange sorbet (page 234) each has its own season. Karen DeMasco, Craft's pastry chef, has devised a formula that I especially like that can be applied by the home cook to nearly every fruit in the marketplace.

Simply stated, Karen makes sorbet by puréeing fruit, adding simple syrup (generally half the amount—$1/2$ cup syrup for 1 cup of purée), and processing the mixture in an ice cream maker. Differences in the natures of the fruit dictate slight variations in this basic method. Some fibrous fruit (blood oranges, for example) are juiced rather than puréed. And some fruits (those with lots of nice sweet liquor like pineapple and berries) are macerated

with sugar overnight then puréed with their sweetened juices. In this case less simple syrup is added.

In the following recipes you'll note that Karen also applies a consistent cooking method to pan-roasting fruit (see pages 218 and 219) and making fruit compotes (see page 236 to 239). The techniques remain the same—all that changes are the fruits themselves, whose different characteristics determine how they are handled and how long they should cook. Whatever you decide to make—sorbet, compote, or roasted fruit—choose fresh fruit in season and at the peak of its ripeness and you're guaranteed an exceptional finish to your meal.

Banana sorbet

THIS DISH IS AN EXAMPLE *of how a good sorbet can have even more intense flavors than the original fruit. Banana sorbet is so creamy, it could pass for ice cream. Try pairing it with Caramel Sauce (page 246) or the Banana Upside-down Cake (page 195). Or both.*

Makes just under 1 quart

2 POUNDS VERY RIPE BANANAS

ABOUT 1¼ CUPS SIMPLE SYRUP
(*page 266*)

JUICE OF ½ LEMON

Peel then purée the bananas. Strain the purée and measure it. Combine the purée with half its volume of simple syrup and the lemon juice, then chill. Process the sorbet in an ice cream maker according to the manufacturer's directions. Transfer the sorbet to containers and freeze for at least 2 hours before serving.

Pineapple sorbet

THIS BASIC SORBET *technique will work well with a variety of fruit (see page 229 for a discussion of the technique). Whichever fruit you choose—strawberries, nectarines, rhubarb—be sure to taste the macerated fruit–sugar mixture for sweetness before adding the simple syrup. Obviously, tarter fruit like rhubarb will need more than some of the others.*

Makes about 1 quart

9¾ CUPS COARSELY CHOPPED
PINEAPPLE (*about 1¹/₂ medium
pineapples*)

6 TABLESPOONS SUGAR

1½ CUPS SIMPLE SYRUP
(*page 266*), OR TO TASTE

Combine the pineapple and sugar in a bowl. Cover and macerate in the refrigerator overnight. Purée the sweetened pineapple mixture in a blender. Strain the purée through a fine sieve. Add simple syrup to taste, then chill thoroughly.

Process the mixture in an ice cream maker according to the manufacturer's directions. Spoon the sorbet into containers and freeze for at least 2 hours before serving.

Concord grape sorbet

CONCORD GRAPES *appear just as Indian Summer turns to fall in September. They have a beautiful blue-black color, sometimes dusted with a silvery bloom that is a sign of freshness. Sorbet is a great way to enjoy the Concord grape's superior flavor while avoiding the seeds. And although it's always a good idea to taste a fruit purée before adding sugar, it's especially important with Concord grapes, which can vary widely in terms of sweetness.*

Makes about 1 quart

3 POUNDS CONCORD GRAPES

¼ CUP SUGAR

1¼ CUPS SIMPLE SYRUP (*page 266*), OR TO TASTE

Wash and stem the grapes. Combine the grapes and sugar in a bowl. Cover and refrigerate overnight. Purée the macerated grapes and their juices in batches in a food processor (it is not necessary to seed them). Strain the purée through a fine sieve and combine it with simple syrup to taste. Chill the mixture thoroughly, then process in an ice cream maker according to the manufacturer's instructions. Transfer the sorbet to containers and freeze for at least 2 hours before serving.

Blood orange sorbet

THE SEASON FOR THESE *beautiful, vivid oranges begins around Thanksgiving and lasts through March. Blood oranges are no longer found only in specialty markets; our pastry chef, Karen DeMasco, reports finding them in her neighborhood market in Brooklyn. Try serving with lemon verbena ice cream (see headnote, page 223) and Almond Biscotti (page 204).*

Makes about 1 quart

2½ CUPS BLOOD ORANGE JUICE
(*juice of about 12 oranges*), CHILLED

1¼ CUPS SIMPLE SYRUP (*page 266*)

Strain the juice and add it with the syrup to an ice cream maker. Process the mixture according to the manufacturer's instructions. Transfer the sorbet to containers and freeze for at least 2 hours before serving.

Sour cherry sorbet

SOUR CHERRIES *have a bright acidity that works well for baking and for sorbet. Be sure to taste the purée–corn syrup mixture before adding simple syrup, as sweetness varies.*

Makes about 1 quart

3¾ CUPS PITTED SOUR CHERRIES (*about 1½ pounds unpitted*)

¼ CUP SUGAR

ABOUT ¾ CUP CORN SYRUP

¾ CUP SIMPLE SYRUP (*page 266*), OR TO TASTE

Combine the cherries and sugar in a bowl. Cover and macerate in the refrigerator overnight. Transfer the cherries and their juices to a blender and purée. Measure the purée and add one quarter the volume of corn syrup. Then taste the mixture and add an equal amount of simple syrup. Chill the purée thoroughly, then process it in an ice cream maker according to the manufacturer's instructions. Spoon the sorbet into containers and freeze for at least 2 hours before serving.

Blueberry compote

FRESH FRUIT COMPOTES work best as a side dish. Try this alongside a simple pastry like Almond Pound Cake (page 193) or spooned over lemon verbena ice cream (see headnote, page 223).

Makes about 2 cups

4 CUPS BLUEBERRIES

¼ TO ½ CUP SUGAR (*depending on the sweetness of the berries*)

1 LEMON

Combine 2 cups of the berries and ¼ cup of the sugar in a saucepan. Simmer over medium heat, stirring gently, until the sugar melts and the berries begin to release their juices, about 3 minutes. Taste the compote and add lemon juice to taste and more sugar if needed. Continue cooking until the berries are soft and the juices syrupy, about 2 minutes more. Remove the compote from the heat and fold in the remaining 2 cups of berries. Serve warm or at room temperature.

Raspberry compote

THIS COMPOTE IS DELICIOUS *spooned warm over Vanilla Ice Cream (page 223).*

Makes about 2½ cups

4½ CUPS RASPBERRIES

¼ TO ½ CUP SUGAR (*depending on the sweetness of the berries*)

Combine 2 cups of the berries and ¼ cup of the sugar in a saucepan and simmer over medium heat until the berries begin to break up, 3 to 5 minutes. Taste the compote and add more sugar if needed. Continue cooking until the berries are soft and the juices syrupy, a minute or so, then remove the compote from the heat and fold in the 2½ cups of uncooked berries. Serve warm or at room temperature.

Apricot compote

ALTHOUGH APRICOT COMPOTE *is served as a dessert at Craft,
I especially love it spread on my toast at breakfast.*

Makes about 2 cups

4 CUPS PITTED APRICOTS

ABOUT 1¼ CUPS SUGAR

JUICE OF ½ LEMON

Combine the apricots, sugar, and lemon juice in a bowl and macerate overnight. Transfer the mixture to a saucepan and bring to a boil over high heat. Reduce the heat to medium and simmer the apricots until they are soft, about 5 minutes. Strain the apricots, returning the liquid to the pan. Reserve the apricots. Simmer the liquid until it is reduced to a syrup (it will feel tacky), then add the apricots. Allow the compote to cool before serving.

Sour cherry compote

As with the apricot compote, *the sour cherries are macerated in sugar overnight, then cooked until tender. The cherry juice is reduced to syrup before the fruit is reincorporated into the dish.*

Makes about 3 cups

5 CUPS PITTED SOUR CHERRIES
(*about 2¹/₂ pounds unpitted*)

3 CUPS SUGAR

Combine the cherries and sugar in a bowl. Cover and macerate in the refrigerator overnight. Pour the cherries and their juices into a saucepan and bring to a simmer over medium-high heat. Reduce the heat to medium and simmer until the cherries are soft, about 7 minutes. Strain the cherries, setting them aside and returning the juices to the pan. Bring the cherry juices to a boil over high heat and reduce until syrupy. Remove the pan from the heat and add the reserved cherries. Serve warm or at room temperature.

Caramel popcorn

KAREN DEMASCO, *Craft's pastry chef, likes to send a small bowl of caramel popcorn, along with Peanut Brittle (page 242) and Strawberry Jellies (page 243), as a parting gift to guests. These delicious confections seem to strike a chord with young and old alike.*

Makes 8 cups

1 TO 2 TABLESPOONS PEANUT OIL

½ CUP POPCORN KERNELS

2 CUPS SUGAR

2 TABLESPOONS UNSALTED BUTTER

1 TABLESPOON KOSHER SALT

1 TEASPOON BAKING SODA

Heat the oil over medium-high heat in a lidded pot. Add the popcorn and cook, shaking the pan frequently, until the popcorn stops popping. Transfer the popcorn to a very large oiled bowl.

Place the sugar in a large saucepan and dampen with about 2 tablespoons water (enough so the mixture looks like damp sand). Add the butter and salt and heat over high, swirling occasionally, until the sugar is melted and the caramel is amber. Remove the pan from the heat and stir in the baking soda.

Pour the hot caramel over the popcorn and carefully stir with a heat-proof spatula until the caramel is evenly distributed and beginning to cool. Cool to room temperature, stirring occasionally, then serve or store in a covered container.

Peanut brittle

At Craft we use salted peanuts to make peanut brittle—this gives the candy a much more lively flavor. I like to send a small bowl of peanut brittle out to guests after their meal, even when they insist they're too full to eat another bite. Somehow the bowl always comes back to the kitchen empty. Keep the brittle in an airtight container; humidity can cause it to lose its crunch.

Makes one 10 x 15-inch pan

2 CUPS SUGAR

¼ POUND UNSALTED BUTTER

6 TABLESPOONS CORN SYRUP

½ TEASPOON BAKING SODA

¾ POUND SHELLED DRY-ROASTED, SALTED PEANUTS

1½ TEASPOONS SALT

Line a rimmed baking sheet with a non-stick baking pad (or lightly but completely oil the sheet). Combine the sugar, butter, corn syrup, and 1⅓ cups water in a large pot. Heat over high until the sugar melts and the caramel turns amber. Stir in the baking soda, then remove the pot from the heat and add the peanuts and salt. Mix well, then, using a metal spatula, quickly and evenly spread the mixture out on the baking sheet. Allow the brittle to cool and harden. Break the brittle into pieces and serve, or store in a covered container.

Strawberry jellies

THIS RECIPE MAKES *over 250 1-inch-square jellies. The recipe works equally well with apples or Concord grapes.*

Ingredients	Method

For the purée

6 quarts	STRAWBERRIES, *stemmed, puréed, and strained*
13 ounces	STRAINED APPLE JUICE
1 cup	GLUCOSE
7½ cups	SUGAR

Combine the strawberry purée, apple juice, glucose, and 7½ cups sugar in a saucepan and bring to a boil.

For the pectin

¾ cup	SUGAR
5 tablespoons	PECTIN POWDER

Combine ¾ cup sugar and the pectin in a bowl. Temper the pectin with a little of the hot purée. Whisk the tempered pectin into the remaining purée. Bring the purée–pectin mixture to a rolling boil. Boil for 1 minute, then pour into two 16 × 12-inch rimmed baking sheets. Cool completely, then cut in inch squares.

For the sugar coating

1 cup	SUGAR
1 teaspoon	CITRIC ACID

Roll the jellies in the sugar coating before serving.

Chilled Sauternes sabayon

TRADITIONAL SABAYON is an airy whisked preparation of egg yolks, sugar, and marsala wine. At Craft we substitute Sauternes—the famous sweet wine of Bordeaux. Once the cream is added, the sabayon can be refrigerated for up to 4 hours.

Makes about 6½ cups

6 EGG YOLKS

SMALL PINCH OF KOSHER SALT

¾ CUP SAUTERNES

6 TABLESPOONS SUGAR

1¼ CUPS HEAVY CREAM

Whisk the egg yolks with the salt, Sauternes, and sugar in a metal or heat-proof glass bowl. Set the bowl over simmering water and whisk until the mixture is thick and the whisk begins to leave a trail, about 20 minutes. Allow the sabayon to cool to room temperature, then cover it directly with plastic wrap and chill thoroughly.

Whip the cream until it can hold soft peaks. Fold the whipped cream, half at a time, into the chilled sabayon. Serve the sabayon alone or with fruit.

Chocolate sauce

Makes about 1 $^1/_3$ cups

¼ POUND BITTERSWEET
CHOCOLATE

½ CUP HEAVY CREAM

¼ CUP MILK

2 TABLESPOONS CORN SYRUP

¼ TEASPOON VANILLA EXTRACT

SMALL PINCH OF KOSHER SALT

Chop the chocolate and place it in a large heat-proof bowl. Combine the cream, milk, corn syrup, vanilla, and salt in a saucepan and bring to a simmer over medium-high heat. Pour a third of the milk mixture over the chocolate and whisk until the chocolate is largely melted. Whisk the remaining milk mixture into the chocolate. Serve warm.

Caramel sauce

ADDING THE BUTTER *to the caramel then adding the cream then the crème fraîche ensures that the sauce doesn't break. Caramel sauce can be made ahead and reheated in a double boiler. It's a natural over Vanilla Ice Cream (page 223) or Banana Upside-down Cake (page 195).*

Makes about 1 1/2 cups

1 CUP SUGAR

2 TABLESPOONS CORN SYRUP

4 TABLESPOONS (½ STICK) UNSALTED BUTTER, DICED

½ CUP HEAVY CREAM

2 TABLESPOONS CRÈME FRAÎCHE

¼ TEASPOON KOSHER SALT

1½ TEASPOONS VANILLA EXTRACT

Place the sugar in a saucepan and add about 2 tablespoons water (enough so the mixture looks like damp sand). Add the corn syrup and cook over high heat, swirling the pan occasionally, until the sugar is melted amber. Remove the pot from the heat and whisk in the butter, a piece at a time. Whisk in the cream, then the crème fraîche, salt, and vanilla. Serve warm.

Passion fruit sauce

Passion fruit were named by Spanish conquistadores, who believed the plant to resemble Christ's crown of thorns, the symbol of his "passion" or crucifixion. Once rare and expensive, passion fruit are now cultivated domestically, making them easier to find in good gourmet stores and supermarkets. The fruit's bright, tangy pulp makes an excellent sauce for Coconut Panna Cotta (page 209).

Makes about 1¹/₂ cups

6 PASSION FRUIT

ABOUT 6 TABLESPOONS SIMPLE SYRUP (*page 266*)

Cut the passion fruit in half and scoop the pulp (including the seeds) into a bowl.

Sweeten the pulp to taste with simple syrup and mix well.

pantry

White chicken stock   250

Brown chicken stock   251

Veal stock   252

Fumet   253

Blonde soffritto base   255

Aïoli   256

Mostarda   257
(*mustard fruits*)

Lemon confit   258

Garlic confit   259

Roasted garlic   260

Ramp butter   260

Green olive tapenade   261

Pan-roasted diced
    vegetables   263

Salsa verde   264

House vinaigrette   265

Truffle vinaigrette   265

Simple syrup   266

Puff pastry   267

8.

White chicken stock

Makes about 5 cups

4 POUNDS CHICKEN LEGS, WINGS, AND BACKS

1 ONION, PEELED AND QUARTERED

1 CARROT, PEELED AND COARSELY CHOPPED

2 CELERY STALKS, COARSELY CHOPPED

2 LEEKS, TRIMMED, WHITE PARTS ONLY, CHOPPED

3 TO 4 SPRIGS OF FRESH FLAT-LEAF PARSLEY

3 TO 4 SPRIGS OF FRESH THYME

Remove the skin and any obvious fat from the chicken. Place the chicken in a large pot, cover with cold water, and bring to a boil. Drain the chicken and rinse out the pot. Return the chicken to the pot and cover with fresh water. Bring to a simmer over medium heat. Simmer, skimming as necessary, until the stock tastes like chicken, about 2½ hours.

Add the onion, carrot, celery, and leeks. Simmer for about 30 minutes, then add the parsley and thyme. Simmer for 10 minutes more. Strain the stock, cool, then remove any fat. Freeze for up to 6 months or refrigerate for up to a week.

Brown chicken stock

Makes about 10 cups

8 POUNDS CHICKEN LEGS, WINGS, AND BACKS

3 TABLESPOONS PEANUT OIL

2 ONIONS, PEELED AND QUARTERED

2 CARROTS, PEELED AND COARSELY CHOPPED

4 CELERY STALKS, COARSELY CHOPPED

4 LEEKS, TRIMMED, WHITE PARTS ONLY, CHOPPED

1½ TABLESPOONS TOMATO PASTE

1 BUNCH FRESH FLAT-LEAF PARSLEY

1 BUNCH FRESH THYME

Heat the oven to 400°F. Remove the skin and any obvious fat from the chicken. Heat the oil over medium-high heat in a roasting pan or very large ovenproof skillet. Add the chicken, skin side down, and cook for about 5 minutes. Transfer the pan to the oven and roast, stirring occasionally, until the chicken begins to brown, about 20 minutes. Add the onions, carrots, celery, and leeks and continue roasting until the chicken and vegetables are well browned, about 30 minutes.

Stir in the tomato paste and roast about 5 minutes more.

Transfer the chicken and vegetables to a large pot, cover with water, and bring to a simmer over medium heat. Cook, skimming occasionally, until the stock is rich and flavorful, about 2½ hours. Add the parsley and thyme and cook about 10 minutes more. Strain, cool, and remove any fat. Refrigerate the stock for up to 1 week or freeze for up to 6 months.

Veal stock

AT MY RESTAURANTS *I like to braise meats in reductions of themselves—rabbits in rabbit stock, chicken in chicken stock. But perhaps the most versatile and widely used stock at Craft is veal stock. Veal has more gelatin than most meat, making its stock a more unctuous base for sauces and an especially delicious braise for short ribs (see page 60).*

Makes about 12 cups

5 POUNDS VEAL BONES

2 TABLESPOONS TOMATO PASTE

2 YELLOW ONIONS, PEELED AND CHOPPED

3 CARROTS, PEELED AND CHOPPED

3 CELERY STALKS, PEELED AND CHOPPED

1 BAY LEAF

3 SPRIGS FRESH THYME

10 BLACK PEPPERCORNS

Place the bones in a large pot. Cover with cold water and bring to a boil over high heat. Drain the bones, discarding the water. Replace the bones in the pot. Again add cold water to cover and the tomato paste. Bring to a simmer over medium heat, skimming any fat or froth that rises to the surface. Simmer the bones, skimming occasionally, for 4 hours, adding water if necessary to keep the level above the bones. Add the onions, carrots, celery, bay leaf, thyme, and peppercorns and simmer for 1½ hours more. Strain, cool, and remove any fat. Refrigerate the stock for up to 1 week or freeze for up to 6 months.

Fumet

FUMET IS A RICH *fish stock that we use at Craft as a base for barigoule. You can order fish heads ahead of time from your fish market; be sure they smell fresh and are cleaned of any blood and viscera before you start. It's important not to stir or agitate the fish heads once you add them to the pot, as this will cloud the stock. Cloudy stock will taste fine but will lack the clarity and visual appeal of a well-made fumet.*

Makes about 1 quart

1 TABLESPOON EXTRA-VIRGIN OLIVE OIL

2 WHITE ONIONS, PEELED AND SLICED

1 FENNEL BULB, CORED AND SLICED

3 CELERY STALKS, SLICED

1 GARLIC CLOVE, PEELED AND CRUSHED

2 BASS OR OTHER LEAN WHITE FISH HEADS, EYES AND GILLS REMOVED

2 CUPS DRY WHITE WINE

2 SPRIGS FRESH TARRAGON

2 SPRIGS FRESH THYME

1 BAY LEAF

8 WHITE PEPPERCORNS

Heat the oil in a large pot over medium heat. Add the onions, fennel, celery, and garlic and cook, stirring occasionally, until the vegetables begin to soften, about 10 minutes.

Meanwhile, soak the fish heads in several changes of water to remove any traces of blood, then add them to the pot. Cover and steam for 15 minutes. Add the wine and simmer, uncovered, until the wine has reduced by half, about 15 minutes. Add the tarragon, thyme, bay leaf, and peppercorns, then add water to cover, about 2 quarts.

Simmer the stock gently without stirring over medium-low heat until the flavors are clear, about 25 minutes. Ladle the stock through a fine sieve. Refrigerate for up to 3 days or freeze for up to 6 months.

Soffritto is a multi-purpose flavoring base used extensively in Italy. It is made by cooking onion, carrot (or fennel), and celery in olive oil. It can be cooked in large batches ahead and refrigerated or frozen.

At Craft, soffritto is used to flavor Romano beans, veal, rabbit, and monkfish, among other things. A slightly different type of soffritto is used for each dish. Cooks at Craft break their many soffritto into three basic categories: blonde, amber, and dark. This is a reference to the extent to which the vegetables are browned. Mild dishes rely on a blonde soffritto—vegetables cooked to the color of straw. Moderately assertive flavors call for an amber soffritto—vegetables cooked to the color of cream soda; and rich meaty dishes begin with a dark soffritto—vegetables cooked to the color of chocolate (not charcoal; dark does not equal burned).

The dish to be prepared determines the degree to which the vegetables are cooked. It also commands what else is added to the soffritto. Peperoncini (Italian dried hot peppers), oregano, and tomatoes are frequent additions, but not always in the same quantities. Rosemary, garlic, wine, and stock are also common enhancements. There are no hard and fast rules about when to add what. Although freedom from rigidly prescribed rules may at first seem a little scary, this flexibility becomes quite consoling with a very little bit of experience.

How does all this translate to a home kitchen? Begin by making a batch of blonde soffritto—this will save you considerable effort when it comes time to make dinner. The blonde soffritto then becomes the base for a variety of dishes. For example, warm a tablespoon or two of the base with some garlic, rosemary, and a little tomato to prepare Braised Romano Beans (page 184), or begin with more base, about 2 cups, then add oregano, peperoncini, white wine, lots of tomato, and some stock to make a braising liquid for Braised Monkfish (page 97). Start with 1/4 cup of base, cook until the vegetables darken, then add tomatoes, wine, and plenty of stock to create a braising liquid for breast of veal (see page 62).

The recipe opposite makes more than 4 cups of base and it can be doubled or tripled without ill effect. The amount of olive oil has been reduced from more traditional renditions. Feel free to add up to an additional cup of oil for a richer flavor. If you follow the recipe as written, make sure that the vegetables don't scorch. Stir frequently and add 1/4 cup of water to keep the pan lubricated if the vegetables seem inclined to stick.

Finally, the smaller the vegetables are cut, the better the flavor of the soffritto. At Craft the celery and carrots or fennel are minced in a food processor. The onion, unfortunately, must be cut by hand.

Blonde soffritto base

Makes about 4 cups

4 CUPS MINCED RED ONION

2 CUPS MINCED CELERY

2 CUPS MINCED CARROT OR
FENNEL

1¾ CUPS EXTRA-VIRGIN OLIVE OIL

Combine the onion, celery, and carrot or fennel in a large high-sided skillet. Add the oil and cook over medium heat, stirring occasionally, until the vegetables are the color of straw, about 45 minutes. Use immediately or cool, then refrigerate for up to 1 week or freeze for up to 6 months.

From top to bottom: Dark, amber, and blonde soffrittos.

Aïoli

Aïoli, a garlicky *mayonnaise, makes a great condiment for cold roasted meats or poached fish. At Craft I use it as a dressing for Fingerling Potato Salad (page 171) or served alongside Roasted Fingerling Potatoes (page 170).*

Makes about 3 cups

1 GARLIC CLOVE, PEELED

KOSHER SALT

1 EGG YOLK

3 TABLESPOONS FRESH LEMON JUICE

2 CUPS EXTRA-VIRGIN OLIVE OIL

FRESHLY GROUND BLACK PEPPER

Finely chop the garlic, then mix in a pinch of salt and continue chopping until the mixture forms a paste. Combine the garlic, egg yolk, and lemon juice in a bowl. Whisk to combine, then, while whisking continuously, slowly add the oil in a thin stream. Season the aïoli with salt and pepper and refrigerate until needed.

Mostarda (mustard fruits)

MOSTARDA IS A CLASSIC *Italian chutney made by slow-cooking fruit (in this case citrus peel) and mustard. At Craft we serve this as a garnish for Pan-roasted Foie Gras (page 41). The mustard fruits' complex blend of sweetness, bitterness, and heat makes them a perfect foil to the richness of the liver. The recipe calls for the Mostarda to chill for at least 2 days before you intend to serve it, but you can go ahead and make it even earlier than that; it only improves with age.*

Makes about 2 quarts

5 ORANGES, SCRUBBED

5 GRAPEFRUIT, SCRUBBED

5 LEMONS, SCRUBBED

4 CUPS SUGAR

½ CUP MUSTARD POWDER

1 PEPERONCINO

3 SPRIGS FRESH THYME

½ TEASPOON JULIENNED FRESH HORSERADISH

Using a paring knife, remove the peel (including the pith) of each piece of fruit in 4 large pieces and reserve. Juice the fruit. You will need about 2 cups total (any extra juice can be saved and used for another purpose).

Combine the fruit juice with an equal amount of water in a large saucepan. Add the sugar, mustard powder, peperoncino, and thyme. Bring the mixture to a simmer over medium heat. Cook until the sugar melts and the favors blend, about 20 minutes. Add the fruit peels, reduce the heat to low, and cook until the peels are tender. Add the horseradish and remove the pot from the heat. Cool, then refrigerate for at least 2 days. To serve, chop the peels, then use as an accompaniment for charcuterie or foie gras.

Lemon confit

THIS IS ONE of the most versatile condiments we make at Craft; I like to send it out with oysters, cured fish, tuna—it even works as a piquant side to roasted meat or chicken.

Makes about 1 quart

6 LEMONS

2½ SHALLOTS, PEELED AND MINCED

3 GARLIC CLOVES, PEELED AND MINCED

⅓ CUP KOSHER SALT

3 TABLESPOONS SUGAR

EXTRA-VIRGIN OLIVE OIL

Blanch the lemons in boiling water, rinse them, wipe them clean, and then thinly slice them. Discard the ends and remove and discard the seeds.

Combine the shallots with the garlic. Mix the salt with the sugar. Cover the bottom of a lidded nonreactive container with a layer of lemon slices. Sprinkle the lemons first with a little shallot mixture, then with some salt mixture. Repeat, layering lemons and sprinkling them with the shallot and salt mixtures until the final lemon slices are topped with the last of the salt and shallot mixtures. Cover the container and refrigerate the confit for 3 days.

The confit can be used immediately or covered with olive oil and kept in the refrigerator for at least a month.

Garlic confit

AT CRAFT *the cooks keep a crock of Garlic Confit handy, which they dip into to baste items like chicken and hanger steak, or to flavor potatoes and mushrooms. Garlic confit is mellower than raw garlic; it provides a nice, subtle garlic flavor that won't overwhelm the finished dish. It can be kept for months in the refrigerator.*

Makes about 12

12 GARLIC CLOVES, PEELED

ABOUT 2 CUPS EXTRA-VIRGIN OLIVE OIL

Place the garlic in the smallest saucepan available. Add enough oil to cover, then heat over medium heat until the first bubbles appear. Reduce the heat to low (it should no longer bubble; if it does, put a skillet under the saucepan to diffuse the heat). Cook until the garlic is very soft, about 40 minutes. Cool the confit to room temperature, then store the garlic in the oil in the refrigerator.

Roasted garlic

Makes 8 cloves

8 CLOVES GARLIC, PEELED

Preheat the oven to 350°F. Peel the garlic, wrap it in aluminum foil, and roast until it is soft, about 30 minutes. Roasted garlic can be stored in a sealed container in the refrigerator for at least a week.

Ramp butter

WE MAKE FLAVORED *butter sauces like this one to serve with skate. If ramps aren't available, leeks or chives will also work. Capers are another good choice—the salt and astringency make a nice counterpoint to the creaminess of the fish.*

Makes about 1 cup

1 POUND RAMPS (SEE HEADNOTE)
½ CUP DRY WHITE WINE
¼ CUP VERJUS
¼ CUP CHAMPAGNE VINEGAR

½ POUND UNSALTED BUTTER, CHILLED AND CUT INTO PIECES
KOSHER SALT

Thinly slice the white parts of the ramps (discard the greens). Combine the ramps with the white wine, verjus, and vinegar in a nonreactive saucepan and reduce over medium-high heat until the pan is almost dry. Reduce the heat to low. Whisk in the butter one piece at a time, season with salt, and serve.

Green olive tapenade

TAPENADE IS A TRADITIONAL *Provençal purée made from capers and olives. I prefer the coarser texture of a fine dice, rather than a purée, and at Craft I serve the tapenade alongside Rabbit Ballottine, page 36.*

Makes about ¾ cup

1 CUP PITTED PICHOLINE OLIVES

1 TABLESPOON CAPERS, RINSED

1 ANCHOVY FILLET

1 TEASPOON DIJON MUSTARD

ABOUT 3 TABLESPOONS EXTRA-VIRGIN OLIVE OIL

Cut the olives in a very small, neat dice. Cut the capers and anchovy the same size. Combine the olives, capers, and anchovy in a small mixing bowl. Add the mustard and mix well. Gradually add enough oil just to bind the mixture. Serve or refrigerate for up to 3 days.

Pan-roasted diced vegetables

THIS IS NOT REALLY *a vegetable dish in its own right, but a garnish I use frequently at Craft for dishes like Farro (page 180) and Pan-roasted Sweetbreads (page 38). The vegetables are the same we use to start soffritto, but the vegetables are diced rather than minced; they are meant to be noticeable components in the finished dish.*

Makes about 2 cups

2 TABLESPOONS PEANUT OIL

1½ CUPS SMALL-DICED RED ONION (*about 1 large*)

¾ CUPS SMALL-DICED CARROT (*about 2 medium*)

¾ CUPS SMALL-DICED CELERY (*about 1 large stalk*)

1 TABLESPOON FRESH THYME LEAVES

KOSHER SALT AND FRESHLY GROUND BLACK PEPPER

1 SPRIG FRESH THYME (*optional*)

1 TABLESPOON UNSALTED BUTTER (*optional*)

Heat a large skillet over medium heat. Add the oil, then the onion, carrot, celery, thyme, salt, and pepper. Sauté the vegetables, turning them as you go, until they are tender and golden, about 5 minutes. Add the sprig of thyme, if using. Keep warm in a low oven (or refrigerate then reheat immediately before serving), adding the butter, if desired, just before serving.

Salsa verde

AT CRAFT we serve salsa verde, a traditional Italian condiment, with Roasted Cod (page 86). The parsley mixture in this recipe can be made several hours in advance, leaving the final addition of olive oil and lemon juice until just before serving.

Makes about 1¼ cups

1 CUP CHOPPED FRESH FLAT-LEAF PARSLEY (*about 3 bunches*)

2 TABLESPOONS CAPERS, RINSED AND CHOPPED

2 ANCHOVIES, MINCED

½ TEASPOON DIJON MUSTARD

ABOUT 3 TABLESPOONS EXTRA-VIRGIN OLIVE OIL

JUICE OF ½ LEMON

KOSHER SALT AND FRESHLY GROUND BLACK PEPPER

Combine the parsley, capers, anchovies, and mustard in a bowl. Gradually mix in just enough olive oil so the sauce holds together. Shortly before serving add the lemon juice and adjust the seasoning if necessary with salt and pepper. Using two spoons, form the salsa verde into quenelles.

House vinaigrette

A L T H O U G H   Y O U   C O U L D cut this recipe in half, it keeps well in the refrigerator, and it also makes a nice braising liquid for fish.

Makes about 2½ cups

2 CUPS PLUS 2 TABLESPOONS EXTRA-VIRGIN OLIVE OIL

3 SHALLOTS, PEELED AND SLICED

½ CUP RED WINE VINEGAR

2 TABLESPOONS DIJON MUSTARD

KOSHER SALT AND FRESHLY GROUND BLACK PEPPER

Heat 2 tablespoons of the oil in a skillet over medium heat. Add the shallots and sweat them until they are soft and translucent, about 15 minutes. Put the shallots in a blender. Add the vinegar, mustard, and a little salt and pepper. Purée the shallots, then with the blender running gradually add the remaining 2 cups of oil in a steady stream. Adjust the seasoning if necessary with salt and pepper, then refrigerate until ready to use.

Truffle vinaigrette

T R U F F L E   V I N A I G R E T T E is one of my favorite indulgences with oysters, in place of a more traditional mignonette.

Makes about 1½ cups

1 TABLESPOON TRUFFLE SHAVINGS

3 TABLESPOONS TRUFFLE JUICE

¼ CUP CHAMPAGNE VINEGAR

½ CUP EXTRA-VIRGIN OLIVE OIL

½ CUP GRAPESEED OIL

1 TABLESPOON TRUFFLE OIL

KOSHER SALT AND FRESHLY GROUND BLACK PEPPER

Combine the truffle shavings, truffle juice, and vinegar. Whisk in the olive oil, grape-seed oil, and truffle oil. Season with salt and pepper and serve with raw oysters.

Simple syrup

At Craft we use Simple Syrup to sweeten sorbets and to poach fruit, but it also makes a great sweetener for iced tea.

Makes 1¼ cups

1½ cups sugar

Place the sugar in a saucepan. Add ³/₄ cup water and bring to a rolling boil over medium-high heat. Cook just until the sugar melts, then remove from the heat. Store at room temperature.

Puff pastry

Ingredients	Method

For the dough

1½ pounds   ALL-PURPOSE FLOUR
6 ounces   CAKE FLOUR
1 tablespoon   KOSHER SALT
2¼ teaspoons   SUGAR
6 ounces (1½ sticks)   UNSALTED BUTTER, CHILLED
1¼ cups   ICE WATER

TO MAKE THE DOUGH

Combine the flours, salt, sugar, and butter. Mix until the dough feels pebbly. Add ice water until the dough feels ropey. Turn the dough out onto a table. Shape it into a rectangle and cut in two equal pieces. Wrap each portion in plastic and refrigerate overnight.

For the butter mixture

3¾ ounces   ALL-PURPOSE FLOUR
1½ pounds (6 sticks)   UNSALTED BUTTER, SOFTENED

TO MAKE THE BUTTER MIXTURE

Mix the flour with the softened butter. Divide it into two square portions, wrap in plastic, and chill.

INCORPORATING THE BUTTER

Place a piece of dough on the work surface. Place a chilled butter square in the center of the dough at an angle (it should look like a diamond within a square). Wrap the dough around the butter so it completely covers it. Wrap in plastic and refrigerate. Repeat.

TURNING THE DOUGH

(First and second turns.) Roll one portion of dough into a long rectangle. Fold the bottom third up then the top third over it to form a three-layered square. Turn the dough ninety degrees (it should look like a book with the spine to the left). Roll the dough into a long rectangle identical to the first (it should fill the same space that the original rectangle did). Fold the bottom third up and the top down. Wrap in plastic and refrigerate for at least 2 hours. Repeat.

(Third and fourth turns.) Place the first portion of dough on the work surface with the "spine" to the left. Roll out into a rectangle, fold in thirds, turn ninety degrees, then repeat. Rest the dough in the refrigerator for 2 hours. Repeat.

(Fifth and sixth turns.) Turn each piece of dough twice more, then refrigerate or freeze.

Acknowledgments

The chicken and the egg debate will go on for eternity, but in the category of restaurant cookbooks the order is clear; before *Craft of Cooking*, there was Craft, the restaurant. For their singular dedication and hard work at Craft, I'd like to thank Katie Grieco, Marco Canora, Karen DeMasco, Victor Salazar, Matthew McCartney, Sisha Ortuzar, Jocelyn Morse, and too many more to mention here: namely the managers, servers, host/reservationists, and dedicated kitchen staff whose efforts have made Craft the exceptional place that it is. Among that group, I'd like to especially thank those individuals who took time out of their busy day to give us the behind-the-scenes story of Craft—your insight was invaluable. Thank you to my partners at Craft, who were willing to take it on faith that a restaurant this different could become a success. Thanks also to the hardworking poeple who bring us our dazzling ingredients—farmers, purveyors, and folks at the Greenmarket—so that we can build Craft's mission from there.

Just as running Craft is a daily collaboration among talented people, so was writing Craft's story: Thanks again to Marco and Karen for working so closely with us on the food. Thanks to Bill Bettencourt for his beautiful photography, and Joey "Cappucino" Mikos. Thanks to our talented designer Bob Dahlquist, our editor, Roy Finamore, and the entire team at Clarkson Potter. A special thank you to Cathy Young who brought her incredible work ethic and patient friendship to the table—without her this book wouldn't have happened. And thanks to Lori Silverbush for her magic touch with my voice, and for always being by my side.

Resources

Meat

DRY-AGED STEAKS, HANGER STEAK, VEAL, CAUL FAT, RABBIT

PICCININI BROTHERS
633 Ninth Avenue
New York, NY 10036
212-581-7731
www.piccininibros.com
Game, game birds, poultry, duck, foie gras, rabbit

D'ARTAGNAN
Tel: 800-DARTAGN (800-327-8246), ext. 3
Fax: 973-465-1870
www.dartagnan.com
Artisan lamb, chickens

ALLEN FARM SHEEP & WOOL COMPANY
361 South Road
Chilmark, MA 02535
Tel: 508-645-9064
allenfarm@vineyard.net

SUMMERFIELD FARM
Tel: 540-547-9600
www.summerfieldfarm.com

FISH

FRESH FISH, SMOKED FISH, SHELLFISH, LOBSTER, CAVIAR

WILD EDIBLES
Tel: 212-687-4255
Fax: 212-687-4477

BROWNE TRADING COMPANY
Tel: 800-944-7848
Fax: 207-766-2404
www.browne-trading.com
Fresh, Seasonal Produce

http://starchefs.com/features/farm__fresh/html/index.shtml

www.ams.usda.gov/farmersmarkets/map.htm

MUSHROOMS, TRUFFLES, SPECIALTY PRODUCE (SUCH AS RAMPS)

MARCHÉ AUX DELICES
Tel: 888-547-5471
www.auxdelices.com or *www.dartagnan.com*
staff@auxdelices.com
Truffles and mushrooms

URBANI TRUFFLES AND CAVIAR USA
Tel: 800-281-2330; 718-392-5050
Fax: 718-391-1704
www.urbani.com
urbaniusa@aol.com

PANTRY ITEMS

ARTISANAL OLIVE OIL, AGED BALSAMIC VINEGAR

www.chefshop.com
Sea salt, *fleur de sel,* artisanal polenta

Browne Trading Company
Tel: 800-944-7848
Fax: 207-766-2404
www.browne-trading.com

D'Artagnan
Tel: 800-DARTAGN (800-327-8246), ext. 3
Fax: 973-465-1870
www.dartagnan.com
Dried beans, farro

Anson Mills
1922-C Gervai's Street
Columbia, SC 29201
Tel: 803-467-4122
Fax: 803-256-2463
www.ansonmills.com

DESSERT INGREDIENTS
VANILLA BEANS, SICILIAN PISTACHIO NUTS, FROZEN FRUIT PURÉES, SPANISH CHOCOLATE

S.O.S. Chefs of New York
Tel: 212-505-5813
ates@soschefs.com for e-mail orders
High-quality chocolate and cocoa powder, baking supplies

New York Cake Supplies
Tel: 800-942-2539; 212-675-2253
Fax: 212-675-7099
www.nycakesupplies.com

Index

Note: Page numbers in *italics* refer to photographs.

Aïoli, 256
Almond Biscotti, 204
Almond Pound Cake, 193
Apple Fritters, 200
Apples, Pan-Roasted, 218
Apricot Compote, 238, *238*
Apricot Tarte Tatin, 192
Arctic Char, Cured, *70*, 71
Asparagus, Pan-Roasted, 119

Bananas, Roasted, 220
Banana Sorbet, 230
Banana Upside-Down Cake, *194*, 195
Beans
    Cannellini, 185
    Chickpea Salad, 112–13, *113*
    Cranberry, 186
    Fava, *182*, 183
    Romano, Braised, 184, *184*
Béarnaise Sauce, 54–55
Beef
    Braised Short Ribs, 60–62, *61*
    Braised Veal Breast, 58–59
    Grilled Hanger Steak with Bordelaise
        Sauce, 51, *52*
    hanger steak, buying, 53
    Pan-Roasted Sweetbreads, 38–39
    Porterhouse Steak with Béarnaise
        Sauce and Roasted Marrow Bones,
        54–55, *55*
    Veal Stock, 252
Beets, Roasted, 120, *120*
Beet Salad with Beet Vinaigrette, *108*, 109
beurre fondue, about, 92
Biscotti, Almond, 204
Biscotti, Chocolate, 205
Biscotti, Pine Nut, 206, *207*
Biscotti, Pistachio, 208
Black Truffle, 155
Blonde Soffritto Base, 255
Blood Orange Sorbet, 234
Blueberry Compote, 236
Bordelaise Sauce, 51
Boulangère Potatoes, 164, *165*
Braised meat, poultry, and seafood
    Braised Monkfish, 96–97, *97*
    Braised Rabbit, *64*, 65
    Braised Red Snapper, 95
    Braised Short Ribs, 60–62, *61*
    Braised Striped Bass, 98–99, *99*

Braised Veal Breast, 58–59
Duck Confit, 63
Lobster Braised in Beurre Fondue, 93–
    94, *94*
Braised vegetables
    Black Truffle, 155
    Braised Baby Fennel, 138
    Braised Cardoons, 142
    Braised Carrots, 139
    Braised Endive, 135
    Braised Morels, 154, *154*
    Braised Ramps, 133
    Braised Romano Beans, 184, *184*
    Braised Salsify, *136*, 137
    Braised Spring Peas, 134
    Creamless Cream Corn, *140*, 141
Breads
    Brioche, 201
    Pain Perdu, 202, *203*
Brioche, 201
Broccoli Rabe, Sautéed, 129
Butter
    beurre fondue, about, 92
    clarified, preparing, 195
    Ramp, 258
Butternut Squash Purée, 146

Cake, Almond Pound, 193
Cake, Banana Upside-Down, *194*, 195
Cannellini Beans, 185
Caramel Ice Cream, 226
Caramel Popcorn, 240, *241*
Caramel Sauce, 246
Cardoons, Braised, 142
Carrots, Braised, 139
Carrots, Roasted, 126, *126*
Cauliflower, Pan-Roasted, 121
Celery Root Purée, 147
Celery Root Remoulade, 111
Charcuterie
    Duck Ham, 30, 31
    Foie Gras Torchon, 34–35, *35*
    Porchetta, 32–33, *33*
    Rabbit Ballottine, 36–37
Cherry, Sour, Compote, 239
Cherry, Sour, Sorbet, 234
Chicken, Pan-Roasted, with Chicken Jus,
    44, 45
Chicken Stock, Brown, 251
Chicken Stock, White, 250
Chickpea Salad, 112–13, *113*
Chocolate Biscotti, 205
Chocolate Sauce, 245

Chocolate Tart, Warm, 196–97, *197*
Cinnamon Cake Doughnuts, *198*, 199
Coconut Panna Cotta, 209
cod, buying, 87
Cod, Roasted, 86
Compote, Apricot, 238, *238*
Compote, Blueberry, 236
Compote, Raspberry, 237
Compote, Sour Cherry, 239
Concord Grape Sorbet, 232
Condiments
    Aïoli, 256
    Garlic Confit, 259
    Green Olive Tapenade, 261
    Lemon Confit, 258
    Mostarda (Mustard Fruits), 257
    Ramp Butter, 260
    Roasted Garlic, 260
    Salsa Verde, 264
Confections
    Caramel Popcorn, 240, *241*
    Peanut Brittle, *241*, 242
    Strawberry Jellies, *241*, 243
Confit, Duck, 63
Confit, Garlic, 259
Confit, Lemon, 258
Corn, Creamless Cream, *140*, 141
Crabs, Soft-Shell
    buying, 83
    cleaning, 82
    Pan-Roasted, 80, *81*
Cranberry Beans, 186
cured dishes. *See* Raw/marinated/cured
    dishes
Custard
    Coconut Panna Cotta, 209
    Lemon Steamed Pudding, *210*, 211
    Steamed Toffee Pudding, 212–13

Desserts. *See also* Ice Cream; Pastry;
    Sorbet
    Apricot Compote, 238, *238*
    Blueberry Compote, 236
    Caramel Popcorn, 240, *241*
    Caramel Sauce, 246
    Chilled Sauternes Sabayon, 244
    Chocolate Sauce, 245
    Coconut Panna Cotta, 209
    Lemon Steamed Pudding, *210*,
        211
    Pan-Roasted Apples, 218
    Pan-Roasted Peaches, 219, *219*
    Passion Fruit Sauce, 247

Peanut Brittle, *241,* 242
Poached Pears, 221
Poached Rhubarb, 222, *222*
Raspberry Compote, 237
Roasted Bananas, 220
Sour Cherry Compote, 239
Steamed Toffee Pudding, 212–13
Strawberry Jellies, *241,* 243
Doughnuts, Cinnamon Cake, *198,* 199
Duck Confit, 63
Duck Ham, *30,* 31

Endive, Braised, 135

Farro, 180
Fava Beans, *182,* 183
Fennel, Baby, Braised, 138
Fennel, Shaved, Salad, 110
Fennel Purée, Sea Urchin with, 76, *77*
Fish
    Braised Monkfish, 96–97, *97*
    Braised Red Snapper, 95
    Braised Striped Bass, 98–99, *99*
    cod, buying, 87
    Cured Arctic Char, *70,* 71
    Cured Yellowtail (Hamachi) with
        Lemon-Coriander Vinaigrette,
        68–69, *69*
    Fumet, 251
    Pan-Roasted Skate, *84,* 85
    Pickled Sardines, *72,* 73
    Roasted Cod, 86
    striped bass, buying, 101
    Sturgeon Wrapped in Prosciutto, *88,*
        89
Foie Gras, Pan-Roasted, *40,* 41
Foie Gras Torchon, 34–35, *35*
Fritters, Apple, 200
Fruits. *See also specific fruits*
    Mustard (Mostarda), 257
Fumet, 251

Garlic, Roasted, 260
Garlic Confit, 259
Gelée, Rabbit, 37
Gnocchi, 172–73, *174–75*
Grains
    Farro, 180
    Polenta, 181, *181*
    Porcini Risotto, 159
Grape, Concord, Sorbet, 232
Green Olive Tapenade, 261
Greens
    baby, buying, 107
    Braised Endive, 135

Herb Salad, 106
Mixed Lettuces with House
    Vinaigrette, 104, *105*
Sautéed Broccoli Rabe, 129
Sautéed Lamb's Quarters, 128
Sautéed Spinach, 132
Sautéed Swiss Chard, 130, *131*

Hazelnut Ice Cream, *224,* 225
Herb Salad, 106

Ice Cream, Caramel, 226
Ice Cream, Hazelnut, *224,* 225
Ice Cream, Maple, 227
Ice Cream, Vanilla, 223

Jellies, Strawberry, *241,* 243
Jerusalem Artichokes
    buying and preparing, 125
    Roasted, 124

Lamb, Baby, 46–47
lamb, buying, 50
Lamb Chops, Pan-Roasted, 48–49
Lamb's Quarters, Sautéed, 128
Leek Salad, 114–16, *115*
Lemon Confit, 258
Lemon-Coriander Vinaigrette, 68–69
Lemon Steamed Pudding, *210,* 211
lettuce, baby, buying, 107
Lettuces, Mixed, with House Vinaigrette,
    104, *105*
Lobster Braised in Beurre Fondue,
    93–94, *94*

Maple Ice Cream, 227
Marinated Lobster Mushrooms, 156–57
mesclun, buying, 107
Monkfish, Braised, 96–97, *97*
Morels, Braised, 154, *154*
Mostarda (Mustard Fruits), 257
Mushrooms
    Black Truffle, 155
    Braised Morels, 154, *154*
    buying and washing, 153
    Hen of the Woods, Pan-Roasted, 150,
        151
    Lobster, Marinated, 156–57
    Porcini in Parchment, 158
    Porcini Risotto, 159
    Truffle Vinaigrette, 263
Mustard Fruits (Mostarda), 257

Olive, Green, Tapenade, 261
Onions, Spring, Roasted, 118, *119*
Orange, Blood, Sorbet, 234

Pain Perdu, 202, *203*
Panna Cotta, Coconut, 209
Parsnips, Puréed, 143
Passion Fruit Sauce, 247
Pastry
    Almond Biscotti, 204
    Almond Pound Cake, 193
    Apple Fritters, 200
    Apricot Tarte Tatin, 192
    Banana Upside-Down Cake, *194,* 195
    Brioche, 201
    Chocolate Biscotti, 205
    Cinnamon Cake Doughnuts, *198,* 199
    Pain Perdu, 202, *203*
    Pine Nut Biscotti, 206, *207*
    Pistachio Biscotti, 208
    Puff, 265
    Warm Chocolate Tart, 196–97, *197*
Peaches, Pan-Roasted, 219, *219*
Peanut Brittle, *241,* 242
Pears, Poached, 221
Peas, Spring, Braised, 134
Peas, Sugar Snap, Sautéed, 127
Pickled Sardines, *72,* 73
Pineapple Sorbet, 231
Pine Nut Biscotti, 206, *207*
Pistachio Biscotti, 208
Poached Pears, 221
Poached Rhubarb, 222, *222*
Polenta, 181, *181*
Popcorn, Caramel, 240, *241*
Porchetta, 32–33, *33*
Porcini in Parchment, 158
Porcini Risotto, 159
Pork. *See* Porchetta
Potato(es)
    Boulangère, 164, *165*
    Fingerling, Roasted, 170
    Fingerling, Salad, 171
    Gnocchi, 172–73, *174–75*
    Gratin, 168
    Purée, *166,* 167
    Stewed, 176
    Sweet, Purée, 177
Pudding, Steamed, Lemon, *210,* 211
Pudding, Steamed Toffee, 212–13
Puff Pastry, 265
Puréed vegetables
    Butternut Squash Purée, 146
    Celery Root Purée, 147
    Potato Purée, *166,* 167
    Puréed Parsnips, 143
    Sweet Potato Purée, 177

Quail, Grilled, 42, *43*

Rabbit, Braised, *64, 65*

Rabbit Ballottine, 36–37

Rabbit Gelée, 37

Ramp Butter, 260

Ramps, Braised, 133

Ramps, Pan-Roasted, 117

Raspberry Compote, 237

Raw/marinated/cured dishes

    Cured Arctic Char, *70, 71*

    Cured Yellowtail (Hamachi) with
        Lemon-Coriander Vinaigrette,
        68–69, *69*

    Duck Ham, *30, 31*

    Foie Gras Torchon, 34–35, *35*

    Grilled Squid, *74*, 75

    Marinated Lobster Mushrooms,
        156–57

    Pickled Sardines, *72, 73*

    Porchetta, 32–33, *33*

    Porcini in Parchment, 158

    Porcini Risotto, 159

    Sea Urchin with Fennel Purée,
        76, *77*

Red Snapper, Braised, 95

Rhubarb, Poached, *222, 222*

Risotto, Porcini, 159

Roasted fruits

    Pan-Roasted Apples, 218

    Pan-Roasted Peaches, 219, *219*

    Roasted Bananas, 220

Roasted/grilled meat

    Baby Lamb, 46–47

    Duck Confit, 63

    Grilled Hanger Steak with Bordelaise
        Sauce, 51, *52*

    Grilled Quail, 42, *43*

    Pan-Roasted Chicken with Chicken
        Jus, *44*, 45

    Pan-Roasted Foie Gras, *40, 41*

    Pan-Roasted Lamb Chops, 48–49

    Pan-Roasted Sweetbreads, 38–39

    Porterhouse Steak with Béarnaise
        Sauce and Roasted Marrow Bones,
        54–55, *55*

Roasted seafood

    Pan-Roasted Skate, *84, 85*

    Pan-Roasted Soft-Shell Crabs, 80, *81*

    Roasted Cod, 86

    Roasted Sea Scallops with Scallop Jus,
        78

    Sturgeon Wrapped in Prosciutto, *88,
        89*

Roasted vegetables

    Pan-Roasted Asparagus, 119

    Pan-Roasted Cauliflower, 121

Pan-Roasted Diced Vegetables, 263

Pan-Roasted Hen of the Woods
    Mushrooms, 150, *151*

Pan-Roasted Ramps, 117

Roasted Beets, 120, *120*

Roasted Carrots, 126, *126*

Roasted Fingerling Potatoes, 170

Roasted Garlic, 260

Roasted Jerusalem Artichokes, 124

Roasted Spring Onions, 118, *119*

Romano Beans, Braised, 184, *184*

Sabayon, Chilled Sauternes, 244

Salad

    Beet, with Beet Vinaigrette, *108,* 109

    Celery Root Remoulade, 111

    Chickpea, 112–13, *113*

    Fingerling Potato, 171

    Herb, 106

    Leek, 114–16, *115*

    Mixed Lettuces with House
        Vinaigrette, *104, 105*

    Shaved Fennel, 110

Salsa Verde, 264

Salsify, Braised, *136*, 137

Sardines, Pickled, *72, 73*

Sauce. *See also* Compote

    Aïoli, 256

    Béarnaise, 54–55

    Bordelaise, 51

    Caramel, 246

    Chilled Sauternes Sabayon, 244

    Chocolate, 245

    Passion Fruit, 247

    Ramp Butter, 260

Sautéed vegetables

    Sautéed Broccoli Rabe, 129

    Sautéed Lamb's Quarters, 128

    Sautéed Spinach, 132

    Sautéed Sugar Snap Peas, 127

    Sautéed Swiss Chard, 130, *131*

scallops, buying, 79

Scallops, Sea, Roasted, with Scallop Jus,
    78

Sea Urchin with Fennel Purée, 76, *77*

Shellfish

    Grilled Squid, *74*, 75

    Lobster Braised in Beurre Fondue, 93–
        94, *94*

    Pan-Roasted Soft-Shell Crabs, 80, *81*

    Roasted Sea Scallops with Scallop Jus,
        78

    scallops, buying, 79

    Sea Urchin with Fennel Purée, 76, *77*

    soft-shell crabs, buying, 83

    soft-shell crabs, cleaning, 82

Simple Syrup, 266

Skate, Pan-Roasted, *84, 85*

soffritto, preparing and using, 254

Soffritto Base, Blonde, 255

Sorbet

    Banana, 230

    Blood Orange, 234

    Concord Grape, 232

    Pineapple, 231

    preparing, 229

    Sour Cherry, 234

Sour Cherry Compote, 239

Sour Cherry Sorbet, 234

Spinach, Sautéed, 132

Squash, Butternut, Purée, 146

Squid, Grilled, *74*, 75

Stewed Potatoes, 176

Stock

    Chicken, Brown, 251

    Chicken, White, 250

    Fumet, 253

    Veal, 252

Strawberry Jellies, *241, 243*

Striped Bass, Braised, 98–99, *99*

striped bass, buying, 101

Sturgeon Wrapped in Prosciutto, *88, 89*

Sweetbreads, Pan-Roasted, 38–39

Sweet Potato Purée, 177

Swiss Chard, Sautéed, 130, *131*

Syrup, Simple, 264

Tapenade, Green Olive, 261

Tart, Warm Chocolate, 196–97, *197*

Tarte Tatin, Apricot, 192

Toffee Pudding, Steamed, 212–13

Truffle, Black, 155

Truffle Vinaigrette, 265

Vanilla Ice Cream, 223

Veal

    Breast, Braised, 58–59

    Pan-Roasted Sweetbreads, 38–39

    Stock, 250

Vegetables. *See also specific vegetables*

    Blonde Soffritto Base, 255

    Pan-Roasted Diced, 263

    for soffritto base, 254

Vinaigrette, Beet, 109

Vinaigrette, House, 265

Vinaigrette, Lemon-Coriander, 68–69

Vinaigrette, Truffle, 265

Yellowtail (Hamachi), Cured, with
    Lemon-Coriander Vinaigrette,
    68–69, *69*